The Expert's Guide to Internet Research

By Eric A. Popkoff, M.B.A.

SPECIALIST PRESS INTERNATIONAL

New York

Specialist Press International books can be purchased for educational, business, or sale promotional use. For ordering details, please contact:

Special Markets Department
Specialist Press International-SPI Books
99 Spring St. • New York, NY 10012
(212) 431-5011 • sales@spibooks.com

For futher information, contact:

New York

S.P.I. Books
99 Spring St., 3rd Floor
New York, NY 10012
(212) 431-5011 • Fax: (212) 431-8646
E-mail: publicity@spibooks.com
www.spibooks.com

10 9 8 7 6 5 4 3 2 1

First Edition
Library of Congress cataloging-in-publication data available

ISBN (13): 978-1561718245
ISBN: 1561718246

The Expert's Guide to Internet Research

By Eric A. Popkoff, M.B.A.

TABLE OF CONTENTS

DEDICATION

I dedicate this book to my brother Sam Popkoff, Chaya and Esther Lichtenstein (two of my best and most helpful students), Richard and Claire Korn, Robert Churbuck, who helped me with the legal aspects of this book; John Adlersparre, whose wonderful cartoons and sage advice added so much to this book; and to my publisher, Ian Shapolsky of Specialist Press International, who believed in this work and the sequels I am planning.

Additionally, I dedicate this book to my wife Lauren, who spent countless long hours typing, revising, and editing this book after many full days of work. Without her help this project would not have been possible.

And lastly, this is dedicated to all the Internet researchers throughout the world.

INTRODUCTION

"The Internet is like a giant jellyfish. You can't step on it. You can't go around it. You've got to get through it."

—John Evans

When surfing the Net, chances are you have either clicked here and there or followed a random trail of what interested you. At times, your search has probably seemed like a scavenger hunt, driven by finding facts in different locations. If this sounds familiar, learning to better use the Internet for research can be among the most useful skills that you can develop.

To a beginner, the Internet can seem to be a large desert, where it is difficult to find anything useful. However, proper Internet research can efficiently help you find your oasis in the desert. Once correctly orchestrated, Internet research can serve myriad purposes, such as company research, research for a term paper or a school assignment, or simply obtaining essential information such as weather forecasts or local/international news.

This book will outline the methods necessary to quickly conduct a proficient Internet search and get all the information you need. It will also include a roadmap that will aid you in your searches, and introduce you to the universe that is the World Wide Web.

When you are doing a serious search on the Internet, mere clicking can get you so confused or overwhelmed that you may lose track of what you were after in the first place. Additionally, you can lose track of time and waste hours on fruitless searching. To avoid this trap you need both a plan for searching and the knowledge to search in the right places.

The first step to an effective Internet search is familiarity with the terms you are searching for. Your search terms should be as concise as possible, while still covering the topic that you would like to find. You should attempt to isloate keywords (main topics), phrases, and terms that describe your area of search. When possible, the search should use nouns and pronouns as keywords, with the most important terms being placed first.

Many search engines operate using a search technique known as "Boolean searching," where operators search for commonality in search terms and include the terms "and," "or," and "but," among other words. A good search should be stated in the terms that you are looking for. Placing the search term in quotes asks the search engine for a match only based on the terms within the quotes. Unless the search engine selected can accept plain English (which a growing number of search engines can) searching for a term not placed in quotes would result in a search for every term in the search box, and would not lead to an efficient search. For example, if you searched for Small Island Developing Nations and Commodities, instead of enclosing the phrase in quotes ("Small Island Developing Nations and Commodities"), you would get results on "Small," "Islands," "Developing Nations," and "Commodities."

In addition to more traditional topics such as News Sources, Internationally based resources, and public records, this book investigates some lesser understood techniques for Internet research. These topics include Really Simple Syndication (RSS), Invisible Web, Web Logs ("Blogs"), and lesser known Government and Library sources.

RSS is a format for publishing news and the content of news-like sites, as well as personal Web logs or Blogs. Almost anything that can be broken down into separate items can be broken down into RSS. RSS aware programs, called news aggregators, are popular in the Web logging community. (News aggregators are discussed in a later chapter.) Many Web blogs make content available in RSS. A news aggregator checks RSS feeds, monitors them, and reacts by displaying changes in each of them.

Given the vast amount of Websites, databases, and programs included in this book, I have developed a rating system that I hope will be of use to the reader. The rating system is as follows:

1 = I could do without it.
2 = Below average in quality, but may have limited use.
3 = Average in scope, but somewhat useful.
4 = Very good, quite useful.
5 = I can't live without it!!

CHAPTER 1:
HISTORY AND CURRENT STATUS OF THE WEB

Adlersparre

B efore one can conduct a true study of the Web, it is vital to know what the Internet itself is all about. The first step is to study the origins and history of the World Wide Web and the Internet. The Internet itself is akin to a large superhighway without any road signs present. It can be considered the digital equivalent of riding the Autobahn at 250 miles per hour, or speeding down Route 66, without knowing where you are or where you are going. Luckily, it is extremely easy to get directions, as there are many available search engines, directories, databases and other aids to help you to find your way around the World Wide Web.

Today, the Internet is populated with millions of sites covering everything from abstract art to zephyrs, and everything else in between. However, this was not always the case. As an observer who has been involved with online databases for over 25 years and the commercial Internet since its inception, I remember it originally being extremely difficult to find much of anything outside of your basic needs. This is due in part to the fact that the Internet was actually slated for an entirely separate purpose aside from information sharing and commercial exchange.

In actuality, no one really "invented" the Internet (not even Al Gore!). The Internet came about as a result of several developments that took place in the early 1960s. In 1961, Leonard Kleinrock at MIT published the first paper on packet switching theory. This theory described the primary method of information transmission over the Internet and was the first step that allowed computers to network. In 1965, Lawrence G. Roberts, working with Thomas Merrill, connected the first computers from two different distance sites together using a low speed dial up telephone line.

The Internet - then known as ARPANET - was brought on line in 1969 to connect four major computers at southwestern universities. The Cold War was still a "hot" topic in the late 1960s, especially as it was coupled with the escalating Vietnam War, and this network was designed to work even if some of the key military and civilian sites were destroyed by nuclear attack. The Government likely believed that in the event of a nuclear attack, universities could provide assistance in solving the myriad problems that would result. This new Internet system would thus be of great use for the Government and military to communicate vital information to universities, think tanks, and other parties.

The early Internet was primarily used by computer experts, the military, and other assorted "techno geeks," and thus lacked any high degree of user friendliness. One of its major problems was with electronic mail transmission, known to us today as e-mail. E-mail was adapted for ARAPANET in 1972. E-mail has advanced tremendously since then. Today's E-mail systems are quite complex, and include vast amounts of storage in addition to other features, such as searching, sorting, and categorization.

The Telnet Protocol, which enabled remote login from any computer, was also developed in 1972. 1973 saw the establishment of the File Transfer Protocol (FTP), which enabled file transfer between remote Internet sites and transmittal of data between computers. The Internet continued to mature quickly throughout the 1970s as a result of an additional architecture known as Transmission Control Protocol/Internet Protocol (TCP/IP). These protocols are still used today to connect active hosts on the Internet.

Started in 1979, USENET allowed the formation of news groups and discussion groups that provided a means of communication over the Internet for those with similar interests. Though USENET is technically considered a separate system from the Internet, most users operate it in conjunction with other Internet based tools. USENET can also be considered a precursor to the "Blogs" of today.

By 1979 modems were running between 100 and 300 bites per second (bps), a far cry from our current speeds (56,000 bps minimum). This was slow but adequate, as there was very little traffic on the networks. I fondly remember becoming a member of one of the first commercial databases in 1979 known as Dow Jones News Retrieval or DJNR. It is hard to realize, considering the content rich Internet of today, how really sparse and unattractive this early system was. The only information that was available was rudimentary: delayed stock quotes, business news, and weather, all in crude black and white, with no graphics. Additionally, by today's standards, the cost for this service was astronomical. Being online cost $20.00 per hour during the day, and $6.00 an hour in the evening, and there was no "all you can eat" pricing for databases at that time.

As the 1980s began, modem speeds increased to about 2,400 bps. This facilitated the appearance of several primitive, but somewhat user friendly sites. In the early '80s, CompuServe was introduced, and is still available, though far less popular today. A few years later, General Electric Information Systems (Genie) introduced their service and Prodigy also appeared. Typically, these sites offered several areas of interest such as news, weather, local information, etc., but were not very graphic in their interface, as modem speeds were simply not high enough to allow for intense graphic content. In addition, members from one service could not e-mail members from another service, as all of these services catered only to their own communities. Later in the 1980s other services were introduced, such as the precursor to AOL, as modem speeds increased into the 4,800 bps range.

Along with these information sharing sites, several of today's most popular services started at this time. The "Chat" platform enabled users to "talk" with each other in real time. Many friendships and even romances started through these Chat services. Almost all major Internet portals have some chat capability. Today "chat" has become a part of our everyday life, and morphed into text messaging, and IM-ing. Chatting capability has advanced beyond the computer to include even phones and other hand held devices.

Around 1990 the true "Internet services" were introduced. The first of these was Delphi Internet, followed shortly thereafter by Pipeline. In the beginning these services were not very well organized or easy to use. The only feature that made them different from their closed service counterparts was the UNIX shell that enabled members to talk with members of other Internet services by e-mail. There was no World Wide Web as we know it today, and information was available in databases scattered all around the Internet. The only search mechanisms available were named Archie, Veronica, and Jughead. These mechanisms searched only for database information and were both complex and very hard to use.

In 1993, modem speeds increased to around 4,800 bps, allowing for some graphics content to be placed on the Internet. This was the very beginning of what is currently known as the World Wide Web, but was sparse and uneven. There were very few available sites, and until the mid 1990s, with the introduction of AltaVista (the first search engine) there was no way to search for World Wide Websites. By 1995, modem speeds had approached 9,600 bps, allowing for rapid explosion of the World Wide Web. Many now familiar sites were introduced at that time, including sites from corporate sponsors, the U.S. Government, and other widely know institutions.

By the end of the 1990s modem speed hit its current maximum dial-up speed of 56,000 [56k] bps. This allowed for an array of new, graphically complex sites. This also led to a new phenomenon called "Pay Per Eyeball." Convinced that they could give advertising content away in return for customers' presence on their site, advertisers drove a flourish of free Web services into development (such as free Web encyclopedias and Internet access), which all featured advertising sponsored content. As time went on, advertisers realized that they were all competing for what was basically the same group of people, and that the response to these ads were not as effective as had been anticipated. Soon thereafter, much of the advertiser based free content disappeared. It was replaced by a pay based model for many of the services and sites.

As the Millennium approached there began the "Golden Era" of the Internet, which led to the dot-com mania of the early 2000s. Many sellers assumed the Internet to be the panacea to solve all of their problems. Just place your products on the Internet and people will buy them. Internet based companies sprang up in droves on the start-up stock markets, and it seemed as if everybody and anybody were rushing to get a commercial Website. New Internet companies sprung up by the thousands, and they would routinely sell for hundred of times their actual market value. Companies lined up at the trade show known as Fall Internet World, and spent obscene amounts of money in an attempt to get recognition from the press, users and the general public. It was almost like the Gold Rush of the 1840s, where a few successful miners sparked a digging frenzy for money hungry individuals, all of whom were panning the same revenue stream for increasingly smaller nuggets. Over time, companies realized that even though the Internet was a very useful tool to transmit information and get customers for their goods and services, it was no magic elixir for a poor idea, product or service. After the shake-out, the remaining companies realized that "eyeball" based advertising models or mere existence on the Net would not create success.

The Web has continued to evolve and we now see a large number of companies that have a presence on it. Many companies have realized that the Web is a useful way to provide information to their established customers, and to gain prospective customers. Additionally, companies such as Amazon.com and E-Bay have created businesses solely based on Web presence. Many companies have also realized that they should mix free and pay services on the same site to maximize their success. Today, savvy companies have developed new and exciting models for Internet sites. Later in this book, we will examine the current uses of the Internet, and what is believed to be the future of the Internet.

Today, we must consider the Internet as basically a gigantic network of interconnected mainframes and computers that can connect to personal computers. The term used for this vast network is "Cyberspace." This is also essentially where the term World Wide Web came from, and its colloquial acronym WWW. This is the hub of large computers transferring data to smaller computers, who in turn are communicating with each other, thus creating a Web-like interface. Even though it is supposed to be infinite in its expanse, as more and more users "log on" to this arena, it sometimes seems as crowded as New York City on Friday at 5:00 p.m., the day before Christmas.

As the demands on the Internet increase, it appears that Cyberspace is attempting to react to the challenge. As time goes on, it is expected that the Web like interface will become increasingly complex and may develop unusual characteristics of its own.

There are many methods that can be used to communicate via the Internet. In "the old days" of the 1970s and '80s, and even the early 1990s, the only practical way to connect to the Internet was through dial-up services. As all of us who have used dial-up know, these services are slow, expensive, and cumbersome.

A dial-up connection needs either a dedicated phone line, which can be expensive, or the patience to faces continuous busy signals, constant disconnections and missed phone calls. Even today, dial-up modem speeds do not exceed those set in the 1990s, a slow maximum of 57,600 bps. At this speed, it is hard, if not impossible, to use much of the content that has become popular on the Web, such as streaming video and graphic interfaces. These various dial-up problems made it obvious that a new, faster method of Internet connection had to be formulated in order to support the newer technologies being developed for Internet use.

Around the year 2000, a small group of Internet service providers (ISPs) began to offer a new service called the digital subscriber line, or DSL. At first this service was hard to find, extremely expensive, not user friendly and not reliable. As time went on prices dropped, availability increased and the service quality became more consistent. This new service and other similar high-speed services were dubbed with a new name, "Broadband."

Following the advent of Broadband, a newer service evolved, with speeds in excess of those known even in industrial quality services. This service cleverly took advantage of the same fiber optic lines already installed for cable TV, and was termed the "cable modem." Cable modem service turned out to be quick, reliable and user friendly, but its downside was its extreme expense to personal home users: in excess of $50.00 a month. To those of us who were weaned on an hourly charged Internet, this may seem rather inexpensive in comparison. Luckily, recent DSL service has now become much more affordable, currently rivaling the cost of standard slower dial-up systems.

The growth and availability of affordable Broadband services has fueled an explosion of new, high band-width content that has become the latest "darling" of the Internet. Among this content are newer, sophisticated games, real time video, and an explosion of personally tailored content that requires this high-speed connection. In fact, it appears that the entire Web is adjusting to cater primarily to those who have Broadband access. AOL, for example, recently offered to provide almost all of their content for free to Broadband subscribers who "brought along" their own connection. This may well be the beginning of a trend that will create an enormous amount of exciting new ad-free content that will only be available to Broadband users. If this is the case, dial-up will likely be on its way to extinction, and the next logical queries will be, "When will Broadband become obsolete?" and, "What will replace it?"

The answer to these questions may lie in a new system known as Wi-Fi. In essence, Wi-Fi is a fast, Broadband based connection that is transmitted by radio from a central computer system to a number of users who share their connection. This is a very different type of connection from the traditional landline Broadband system.

Wi-Fi itself is evolving as you read this book. When Wi-Fi started a few years ago, systems were called B-systems, and allowed only for transmission 100 feet or so from the source. Systems later evolved to G-class, which allowed for transmission up to 300 feet. Now there are 'N' and even larger class networks that may cover areas from a few blocks to an entire city. This has set up the brand new possibility of Internet access without an ISP.

Currently, it seems as if large commercial advertisers are buying and sponsoring large networks in major cities, such as San Francisco. In the near future, it is expected that New York City, its suburbs of Long Island, and Westchester and Rockland counties will be covered by these networks. This system also operates in airports and some other public and commercial areas, where a multitude of personal computers can attach simultaneously to the same Wi-Fi network. Many savvy hotels and motels have also become Wi-Fi zones, although it may cost users money.

The only problem that I see with these developments is the important issue of Wi-Fi security. As anyone who owns a Wi-Fi network knows, it is possible for a hacker to attack even a secured network. I expect that these new networks will eventually be extremely secure, with a yet to be developed encryption scheme.

It is very probable that in the near future the increase of Broadband usage will cause the Internet to be delivered like television, as a free, advertiser-sponsored signal that anyone can use. This will probably lead to an intriguing future device that will act as an all-in-one television/receiver/printer/fax machine, which can deliver content to users upon demand.

One legitimate question that is raised by these new technologies is, "What type of information can I currently get on the World Wide Web?" As of today, the choices are almost limitless, and provide users numerous options. In the entertainment sector alone there is an incredible group of choices. A user can listen to an almost limitless number of Web based radio stations that cover the Internet in almost every available category or style of music, talk, sports, etc. Recently, many television stations have also made their content available on the Web, and there is also a tremendous amount of video and gaming offerings. Additionally, up-to-the-minute news may be viewed on any Internet capable computer. It appears that use of the World Wide Web is only constrained by the limits of the imagination of users and current legal requirements.

Another logical question from a potential user is, "What is NOT available on the World Wide Web?" A good rule of thumb is that content that would be restricted without the presence of the Web would also not be available through the Web. Examples of this type of content are medical records, personal credit records, unlisted phone numbers, bank records, etc. Additionally, content restricted by copyright laws, such as music, commercial movies, and certain computer programs may only be available by gaining a user license and paying an appropriate fee. Unfortunately, a few misguided Web users will always try to beat the system by stealing or illegally transmitting copyrighted or restricted content. Recently, enforcement actions against these few miscreants have been stepped up, and many of these individuals will be next using a computer from inside of a Federal prison.

The next question a user should ask is, "What are the costs of acquiring information on the World Wide Web?" These costs can be broken down into two categories: the cost of acquiring an Internet signal and the cost of acquiring content. Recently the cost of acquiring signal to connect to the Internet has been dropping. DSL services are selling for approximately the same amounts that dial-up did a few years back, and the costs of fast Broadband services are dropping due to competition in the marketplace. Given the future possibility that Wi-Fi service may be offered for free in highly populated areas, and perhaps even nationwide, it appears that Internet access services may also become free via a transition to an advertising-supported platform. The only thing that is certain is that the quality of services will get better and that the costs will continue to decrease.

As far as cost for Web content goes, most information is already available for no charge if ads are incorporated on the site, or if the user is required to register with the site and provide their demographic information. Among the best free content currently available on the Web is AOL, which was recently a pay service. Also free are almost all newspapers, many T.V. and radio stations, interactive chat, interactive games, and a plethora of other application. As I will describe in a later chapter, a substantial amount of pay content is available for free through services such as public and university libraries.

Though it is possible to use a combination of free services to find almost anything you want or need on the Web, there are occasionally items or information that are not available for free by any method. Pay content runs the gamut from extremely expensive, such as the database ORBIT and the legal and news search Website LEXIS-NEXIS, to inexpensive content such as CNN Pipeline (which is actually now free and has been integrated within the main CNN site). Highly specialized content such as LEXIS-NEXIS is primarily used by corporations, private investigators, professional researchers, lawyers, and doctors.

Considering the tremendous amount of valuable free information that is available on the Web, users should truthfully not need to pay a large amount of money for content. For the average individual, there is more than sufficient free content to meet almost every need.

CHAPTER 2:
METHODS OF SEARCHING

There are many different types of search engines that a potential user can access on the Internet, some more popular than others. Popularity, however, may not best serve your needs. Unfortunately, the search engine that you initially choose may not be the optimal one for your intended purposes.

When you have surfed the net, chances are you either clicked here and there or followed a trail of what interested you. This probably resulted in your search becoming a sort of random scavenger hunt with the searcher consumed with finding facts in several different locations. If you can relate to this, learning to optimally use the Internet for research will be the most useful skill that you will develop from reading this book.

To a beginner, the Internet can seem to be a large ocean where it is difficult to find anything useful. However, good Internet research skills will help users to find the port in the stormy sea. Once correctly utilized, efficient Internet research skills can be used for myriad purposes, such as acquiring information on companies, research for a school assignment, or finding information such as weather forecasts or local news. This chapter will outline some of the methods necessary to conduct an efficient Internet search and get the information one needs.

The first step to an effective Internet search is familiarity with the terms you are searching for. Your search terms should be as concise as possible, while still covering the topic that you would like to find. You should attempt to form keywords (main topics), and phrases that describe your topic. When possible, the search should use nouns and pronouns as keywords, with the most important terms being placed first.

As mentioned in the Introduction, many search engines operate using a search technique known as "Boolean searching," where operators search for commonality in search terms and include the terms "and," "or," and "but." Placing the search term in quotes asks the search engine for a match based only on the terms within the quotes. Unless the search engine selected can accept plain English, searching for a term not placed in quotes would result in a search for every term in the search box, and would not lead to an efficient search.

My college students often ask me, "Why can't we get good information from the Internet?" My first response to that question is to ask the student what their search term was. Typically, their search terms selected were either too broad in scope, or not really "on point" for what they wanted to find. A good example came from a student who wanted to know about world oil production and entered the word "oil" as his search term. This led him to such various unhelpful search results such as: baby oil, vegetable oil, or motor oil, and even the movie "Lorenzo's Oil."

The student would have been much better served by beginning a more comprehensive search using a better type of search engine, and searching for "world oil production for 2007."

The first step to an effective Internet search is being familiar with the terms you are searching for. Your search term should be as concise as possible, while still covering the specific area you would like to find. You should attempt to form keywords (the main topic of research), phrases (avoid common phrases unless they are placed in quotes) and terms that describe your topic. The search should use nouns and pronouns as keywords whenever possible, with the most important terms being placed first. As mentioned in Chapter 1, many search engines operate by "Boolean search terms", and include the terms "and, or, and but" among other terms.

A good starting point for effective Internet research is finding an effective search engine from among the many different types that are available. For a standard search engine, some of the most popular include Google (www.google.com), the invisible search engine IncyWincy (www.incywincy.com), the metasearch engine Clusty (www.clusty.com), and the specialized Government search engine www.usa.gov. (See next page.)

Although both the Invisible Web and Meta search engine formats are explained in-depth later on in this book, for the sake of clarity we will define them here as well. Invisible Web search engines search the "hidden" Web for material that is not ordinarily available using the standard search engines. Metasearch engines utilize multiple search engines simultaneously, and filter out redundant results.

Standard search engines such as Google and Yahoo perform many functions in addition to conducting searches. They may be used to look up phone numbers, create maps, report local news and complete other functions. This type of search engine could be considered the "Swiss Army Knife" of the Internet, but unfor-

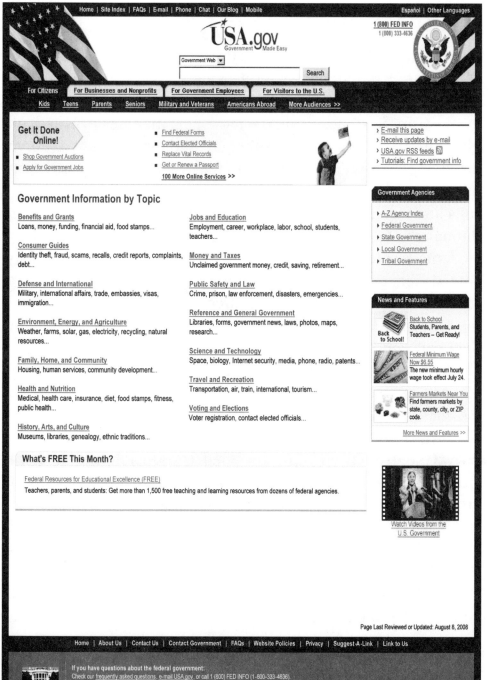

tunately often performs, in my opinion, searches at a mediocre level. Essentially these search engines give you searching capability without the "bells and whistles" of more specialized search engines. A professional researcher would avoid using this type of search engine and would instead use a more suitable search mechanism. Searches using the more general types of search engines also yield many results that are not particularly well organized, or relevant. This can lead to the often frustrating quandary of being unable to find what you need in the first few pages of results and then running out of time or patience before you can go through the additional hundreds of pages of untargeted results.

A metasearch engine, such as www.iseek.com or www.clusty. com, differs greatly in both capability and utility from a general search engine. Although these search engines cannot perform all the functions of the "Swiss Army Knife" general search engine, they can conduct highly efficient searches. Instead of using a single search engine, a metasearch engine uses several search engines and a filter to come up with the best results out of all of the chosen search engines.

To illustrate some of the fundamental differences between www.Google.com and my top rated metasearch engine www. clusty.com, I entered the same term into both, "New York State tax increases." Google returned a whopping 525,000 hits for this topic, many of which were off topic. www.clusty.com, with its superior filtering system, returned 181 hits that were very much on topic.

In addition, some metasearch engines such as www.iseek. com and www.clusty.com have an important feature known as "clustering." In addition to filtering their results, these search engines show the exact subcategories of the search. In the example above, if I only wanted "property tax increases," I could see that only 26 results out of the 181 total correlated directly with this query. This is a great time saver that can zero in on the intended result quickly.

In addition to clustering, many metasearch engines also have relevancy rankings based on the accuracy of the source found to the question asked. For example, if I asked, "Why does a dog bark?" and the first hit was "cat meowing problems" the relevancy ranking for this answer is zero. This lets me know to go on to the next result, without wasting time reading a page that does not address my problem. General search engines, as a rule, do not have this relevancy capability.

Logically, an informed Internet user should ask specific questions about their searches, the first one being: "What do I want as a final result of the search?" While some see this as working backwards, it is in fact a helpful tool for research. In essence, you are focusing on exactly what you want to end up with, rather than asking a more general search question, and letting your search results guide and clarify your final result.

As previously described, search engines with clustering capabilities, such as www.iseek.com or www.clusty.com, prove to be tremendous time savers because it is possible for users to see the subcategories of the initial search. In addition, clustering may lead users to see other useful ideas that were a part of the original search. All in all, it would be preferable to use a metasearch engine over a standard search engine due to its capability of searching through multiple search engines and filtering the results. Therefore, using a metasearch engine will ensure the best results.

Another problem that can develop in a proposed search is: "What happens if I am conducting a search and I find a site I like, but it does not exactly meet the criteria for what I need?" I would like to recommend two available tools that can address this issue, though they are, as of now, only available for Internet Explorer. The first tool is Alexa, available at www.alexa.com. This installs as a toolbar within Internet Explorer, and shows the site rank (how popular the site is in comparison with other sites), as well as sites that are similar in nature to the site you are viewing. This tool is extremely valuable as it allows users to navigate between related sites until a desired result is achieved. Like all Internet explorer toolbars, the use of Alexa reduces available screen space slightly. Most automatic spy ware checkers will warn users that Alexa is spy ware, but this is incorrect.

The second available tool is UCMore, available at www.ucmore.com. This tool, like Alexa, shows sites similar to the one you were examining, but is much more comprehensive. UCMore shows several categories of information related to your chosen search, with several matched sites. This tool is a must for every serious researcher, and significantly more user friendly than Alexa. UCMore looks a little different on the screen than most other toolbars because this toolbar exists on the top right of the Internet Explorer screen, but does not cause Alexa's loss of screen space. The downside of UCMore is that it does not work on as many sites as Alexa does. Most spyware programs also flag UCMore incorrectly.

I have both of these tools installed on my own PC, and I find them to be indispensable in my Internet searches. These tools allow me to perform "semantic" Web related searches, spawned by related items that are developed from your original search. For example, in the search mentioned before on "the world oil production," a semantic Web related search may lead to such search terms as: "OPEC," "Cartels," "Drillers," "War in the Middle East," and "Oil companies." The ability to perform and utilize semantic Webbing is a vital skill to perfect. Using this skill proficiently to perform a challenging and thorough search is a sign of a top flight researcher.

The next useful resource for Internet searching arises via one's Internet Service Provider (ISP). In basic terms the ISP provides the infrastructure for users' connection to the Internet. In the "old days" of dial-up, ISPs had modems connected to mainframe computers, which allowed users to access the Internet. It was therefore virtually impossible to connect to the Internet without an ISP. Today, ISPs provide Internet connectivity via a variety of different methods, including DSL, dial-up, cable modems, satellite, and Wi-Fi. Many ISPs have become well known, such as EarthLink, AOL, MSN and Yahoo.

An ISP not only provides the Internet connection, but usually a number of additional useful services. Almost all ISPs, for example, provide users with E-mail services. As a good rule of thumb, these services will give you an E-mail address with their domain name as a suffix, i.e. epopkoff@pipeline.com. In the past, these ISP driven E-mail accounts were an absolute necessity, since they were the sole way to receive e-mail. Currently, however, there are a large number of providers that provide free or low cost E-mail accounts and thus the relative importance of ISP driven E-mail has diminished.

As an additional service, many ISPs also offer a connection to USENET, which allows users to connect to newsgroups. A newsgroup is basically a special interest group that exchanges posted messages on a variety of topics related to a central subject. A typical newsgroup may be entitled "Domestic travel" and may include many postings on topics such as travel sites, hotels, vacation packages, etc. USENET has now decreased in popularity with the emergence of more sophisticated services on the Web, which provide richer content and better tools.

Due to extreme competition, many ISPs now provide an array of useful services. Among the most popular of these offerings are free firewall and anti-virus programs. These programs, typically provided by the McAfee brand, present the subscriber with free basic protection for the entire computer. ISPs also provide other services such as anti-spy ware protection, anti-spam protection for E-mail, and anti-phishing protection.

In the search for subscribers, ISPs have had to go even further in their attempt to capture new subscribers. AOL, for instance, is not only entirely free to customers, but also includes basic Internet protection software. EarthLink provides gigabytes of free off-line storage, as well as discounts to other well known commercial services. EarthLink also provides anonymous E-mail addresses that protect against potential E-mail third party misuse. The MSN ISP provides free access to many interesting programs, including their own excellent Encarta Encyclopedia program. As the competition for subscribers becomes even more cut throat, it appears that ISPs will be pulling out all the stops and will likely drop their prices in an attempt to sway the few remaining undecided subscribers to their service.

Now for the million dollar question: "Does a user really need an ISP?" The answer almost always depends upon the type of connection that they use with the ISP, dial-up, DSL, or a cable modem. In the near future, with the development of regional and national Wi-Fi systems a possibility, one may be able to connect to the Internet without an ISP. In reality, most users do not really have a need for an ISP service if some other entity provides a reliable Internet connection. Additionally, most of the services traditionally offered by ISPs such as firewall, E-mail, and anti virus software can now be easily acquired for free. Therefore, it is entirely possible that traditional ISP's may become obsolete once broadband Wi-Fi service becomes widely available. All that users would have to provide in order to access these Wi-Fi services is a network card attached to their computer.

In order to achieve the desired results for a search, one of the most important factors that can make or break your efforts is the structure of the search. In this chapter, I have highlighted several methods of effective searching that can be implemented by the reader so that they can achieve an effective search. By implementing these methods it is possible for the searcher to achieve excellent, professional level results with a minimum of time and effort.

CHAPTER 3:
THE INVISIBLE WEB AND HOW TO USE IT

I n today's changing search environment, it is vital to utilize all available tools to achieve an effective and successful search. In most cases the searcher will start with the use of a standard or a metasearch engine. If these search engines do not achieve the desired result, the searcher often gets frustrated and confused about what steps he or she can take to complete a successful search.

A researcher does have other searching resources available even if they are stymied by a standard or metasearch engine. Among professional researchers, much of their searching is performed using the "invisible Web" (also called the "hidden Web" or "deep Web"). The invisible Web encompasses content that is not ordinarily found in most standard or metasearch engines that perform BOT searches for known HTML pages or tags. Most invisible Web content is stored in databases or other similar type of content that cannot be seen by standard search engines. In truth, over 90% of all content on the Web is invisible in nature, "hiding" a tremendous amount of valuable information. In fact, the search company, Bright Planet, estimates that the invisible Web may be up to 500 times larger in scope than the actual Web. The invisible Web is thus a tremendous resource and almost infinite in scope.

A researcher may ask, "Why should I use the invisible Web when I can get most of what I need using a standard search engine?" In reality, most of the information that users will require for performing challenging searches is not available on the standard Web. Because of the nature of the invisible Web, a large amount of the information required to complete a search is "locked up" in areas such as databases. One must exercise caution with these searches however, as results from the invisible Web are like the proverbial "girl with the curl," when they are good, they are really, really good, but when they are bad, they are horrid. In order to conduct effective searches on the invisible Web, a researcher must thus monitor and analyze their results more closely than with more conventional type of search.

Another pertinent question concerning invisible Web searching is, "When is it most useful to the researcher to use this type of search?" A good methodology would be to first study all available results using the old standard search engines and, preferably, the results from the metasearch engines. If the desired result is still not achieved, or supplemental data is still needed to complete the search, then the invisible Web should be utilized.

Typically, invisible Web domains encompass Governmental, organizational, and educational arenas that feature sites with suffixes such as .gov, .org, and .edu. Invisible Web domains can also include commercial databases that may not have Web addresses at all, and may have some pay content. Below, I have listed nineteen search mechanisms that I believe are representative of invisible Web search and available databases. This is not a complete list of sources, but should be used as a representation of some of the available sites that can access the invisible Web. With only one exception, all of the sites that I will mention are free to users, but may require registration or other data to be sent to the service provider. These are also each rated from 1 to 5, with 5 being the highest rating.

INVISIBLE WEB SEARCH ENGINES

1. Copernic, www.copernic.com

This search engine comes in three types, two of which are pay. The basic Copernic search engine is a free download, and is sufficient for most users. In a typical Copernic search, regular Web search results are combined with invisible Web search results. This is a highly regarded search engine due to its comprehensiveness, the effective nature of its metasearch engine filtering system, and its use of Plain English language searching. Copernic is also one of the few search engines that has confidence based ranking to tell you how relevant the results are in relation to your search term. This is an important tool that will save you time. If I ask about a dog, and the results are about a cat, confidence ranking is zero. Copernic searches about 90 search services, each with 10 or more subcategories that include content throughout the Web. Copernic is highly recommended and considered one the best mechanisms of its type on the Web. **Rating=4.5**

2. Incywincy, www.incywincy.com

This search engine provides excellent invisible Web based results. Its system allows users to search specific types of invisible Web categories that might meet the criteria of the search. Among its other features, Incywincy allows for searches with forms. It also tends to have a significantly higher amount of hits per search than a metasearch engine. In my opinion, for those who need an invisible Web search engine, this one is the best that is currently available. If used correctly, it can produce remarkable results. **Rating=4.5**

Web   Forms   Directory

Advanced Search
Preferences
Search   Safe Search Off
Create Account

Learn more about IncyWincy

Powered by Net Research Server ©2007 LoopIP LLC | Listings & Keywords

3. The U.S. Government Search System, www.usa.gov

This excellent site is the master gateway to a full range of Government services on the Federal, State, and Local levels (primarily Federal.) Most of these resources are invisible Web based.

An entire later chapter will be devoted to the description of the Government presence on the Web. **Rating=4.5**

LOCAL LIBRARY-BASED SEARCH SYSTEMS

There are many library based search systems, which allow free access to mostly pay-based, commercial databases for their patrons. There is a tremendous diversity of data available at local libraries, though it varies somewhat from state to state, and system to system. Almost all library databases are invisible Web in nature. The types and uses of the invisible Web databases that are available from libraries will be described in more detail in a later chapter.

1. The Librarian's Index to the Internet, www.lii.org

This comprehensive and searchable index includes over 20,000 Websites, many of which are invisible Web databases. These databases can be accessed by typing in a topic and adding the term "and databases" to it. **Rating=4**

2. Infomine, http://infomine.ucr.edu

This database is a collection of scholarly research primarily focused at the university level. It includes material such as dissertations, theses, publications and other scholarly data. Although this database can be quirky it often produces extremely efficient results in difficult searches. **Rating=3.5**

3. OAIster, www.OAIster.org

OAIster is a project of the University of Michigan, Digital Library Production Service. It has created a collection of academically oriented digital resources easily searchable by every one. OAIster harvests information from many different institutions, and features over 14,900,000 citations. This site certainly is worth a look when you need academic sources. **Rating=3.5**

4. Complete Planet, www.completeplanet.com

This site contains approximately 70,000 searchable databases that are invisible Web in nature. It is considered by many to be a useful resource. **Rating=2.5**

5. Amazon, www.amazon.com

You might not think of a bookseller as a traditional source of invisible Web data. However, Amazon has a search mechanism that allows for the examination of portions of certain books covering a variety of topics and interests. This feature makes Amazon an interesting starting point for invisible Web book related searches. **Rating=4.5**

6. The Internet Public Library, www.IPL.org

A wonderful, relatively unknown source of invisible Web data, as well as library based data; IPL has some subject collections that are listed by category. In addition, IPL hosts prepared reference data and an Internet reading room with a substantial amount of books. You may now "Grok" the IPL results and hit Map View for a visualization of the results. **Rating=4**

7. Refdesk, www.refdesk.com

Refdesk features the Associated Press (AP) news feed and several invisible Web search mechanisms such as directory, Web, business searches and people searches (the latter two are powered by www.whitepages.com). In addition, there are several interesting pieces of data available, such as a thought of the day, a site of the day, and "This day in history." Each of these, upon request, can be made available and included in your daily E-mail. A tremendous amount of invisible Web links are available in categories such as news, photos, gas prices, newspapers, potpourri, etc. **Rating=4.5**

8. Magportal, www.magportal.com

This excellent resource will be discussed in greater length in a future chapter. In essence, Magportal allows user access to a number of magazines, many of which are normally categorized as pay content. Magportal allows for plain English searching, and a large majority of the information returned is in full text format so that the full article may be viewed and printed. Additionally, there is a search mechanism that allows searches for magazine articles that are similar to the article that you are examining. This is a Top 10 site that is an essential resource for any researcher. **Rating=5**

9. Answers.com, www.answers.com

Formerly the pay service known as Gurunet, this is another excellent resource that allows users to access several invisible Web types of search mechanisms, such as a dictionary, an encyclopedia, and other useful related resources. The free, downloadable program also uses very little memory and desktop space. This useful tool allows insertion of search terms via either a small retractable toolbar located on the desk top, a right click of the mouse, or a hot key combination that facilitates finding answers at any point during a search. Answers.com can also send a summary page of the historical events of the day and other useful information directly to the desktop. Answers.com is a must for the serious researcher. **Rating=5**

10. Congoo Netpass, www.congoo.com

This is a relatively new and extremely interesting search mechanism for the invisible Web. The free Congoo tool bar is available for both Internet Explorer and Firefox but to acquire it every user must complete a free registration process. Congoo provides free access to nearly 300 premium content sources, almost all of which are invisible Web in nature. Congoo members may view free articles related to their search every month from each partner site. However, the number of free articles available each month varies by publisher. This allows information gatherers to access information without having to pay for hundreds of subscriptions.

In addition to its primary search capability, Congoo includes an excellent image search that is screened for objectionable content, and categorized and tagged by experts. The images are provided primarily by dozens of professional photo companies. Considering the cost ($0) and the potential benefits from the use of Congoo Net pass, it is a "no brainer" that you should install Congoo Netpass. **Rating=4.5**

11. CEO Express, www.ceoexpress.com

The publisher describes this search engine as "a business portal for executives, created by a busy executive." Regardless of its mission statement, CEO Express is a treasure chest of excellent research links, most of which are invisible Web in nature. I consider CEO Express to be "the invisible Web for dummies," yet at the same time, much more. The basic design of CEO Express is somewhat similar to that of Refdek, but considerably more in-depth. For non business users, there is another site for writers similar to CEO Express located at www.journalistexpress.com.

Among the useful links provided by CEO Express are those for daily news, business news, business magazines, business knowledge, and an excellent list of newsfeeds. This site also links to SECSearch and Answers.com, Online TV News, time and weather, and Technews sites which themselves all feature useful sublinks that lead to hundreds of additional useful resources. With CEO Express, you do not really need to know the categories of search and links. All you have to do is find an area you are interested in, and use the provided link to expand your search. I consider CEO Express to be indispensable because the provider links can solve many researching dead ends. **Rating=4.5**

12. Bartleby, www.bartleby.com

Bartleby is an interesting type of invisible Web resource. It has links to several categories of invisible Web data, such as classic books that are in the public domain. In addition, Bartleby has links to dictionaries, encyclopedias, thesauruses and other scholarly publications. Bartleby's ease of use, and its point and click category interface make it a personal favorite with me and many of my students. **Rating=4**

13. NewsNose, www.newsnose.com

This free search engine can be acquired at www.download.com. Newsnose is a completely unique resource that allows users to conduct sophisticated searches for news. Newsnose allows users to search up to 50 newspapers around the world for up to three combined search terms. Newsnose is a must for news junkies and another top selection. It will be discussed more thoroughly in a later chapter. **Rating=4.5**

14. Questia, www.questia.com

Questia is the only one of the profile services that has any cost associated with its use, and this cost is about $100 a year. This unique invisible Web research source is perhaps the most essential site on the entire Internet for a serious researcher. Questia allows users to access about 65,000 books in all types of categories, all of which they can use and copy as they see fit. Among the books are classics, textbooks, and a plethora of other offerings, most of which are published by middle or small size publishers. In addition to offering the full content of the available books, Questia also includes all of the relevant magazine, journal, and encyclopedia sources that are associated with that current search.

There is one small problem with Questia. It is the fact that Questia conducts searches by Boolean Search Technique. Despite this difficulty, Questia is an unbelievable resource. It is, in my opinion, the top available resource for invisible Web data and is essentially a one stop solution for most invisible Web searches. It is easy to use and can be of use to anyone, from a Middle School student to a Ph.D. candidate. I have used Questia as a textbook substitute in college courses that I have taught and enjoyed remarkable results. Questia is a MUST and an essential resource for any student or researcher. **Rating=5**

15. Argali White and Yellow, www.argali.com

Most researchers would not consider telephone directories as being invisible Web in nature, or being a potentially useful resource. Telephone directories are actually essential when you are performing people searches. Argali is one of the most comprehensive sources of telephone data on the Internet and is second only to the library based Reference USA in total usability.

Argali is a free download that comes in an advertising supported personal edition. It can perform searches for personal and business phone numbers, reverse searches for phone number and street addresses, and searches for toll free phone numbers, maps, area codes, zip codes, and even weather conditions and forecasts. Argali white and yellow aggregates information from at least ten different directories and performs extremely efficient searches of this information I consider Argali white and yellow to be a highly effective tool for any invisible Web researcher and another TOP 10 resource. **Rating=5**

16. Individual, www.individual.com

Individual is a free news clipping service. Most commercial news clipping services cost at least $1000 a month, and in my opinion, are not as useful. Individual allows you to set up your own personal NewsPage where you can tell the site precisely what you want from a side range of business, industry, financial, sports and company specific news. You may also categorize and customize Individual to meet your own interests, and track over 5500 public companies. Individual searches all available news items that cover your selected topics or interests, and then produces a newspaper-like interface that has summaries of each topic and links to the full article. In addition, Individual can be delivered daily, via E-mail, to your personal E-mail address. Individual.com is another TOP 10 site. **Rating=5**

17. Ingenta Connect, www.ingentaconnect.com

Ingenta Connect has over 24 million articles, chapters and reports, from over 31,000 publications, available in its database. Even though a bulk of the content is pay oriented, there is still a substantial amount of content that is free, making this database a great choice for scholarly research. **Rating=4**

In summary, since only ten percent of Web content is available through standard search engines, knowledge of the invisible Web is a vital tool for any researcher. Mastery of the invisible Web is a necessity if one is going to conduct searches on more than a cursory level. I consider a working knowledge on searching the invisible Web to be the most essential Internet research skill.

In this chapter, I profiled twenty useful invisible Web resources culled from hundreds of available candidates. As a general rule, invisible Web research requires more skill, knowledge, and finesse than would be needed to search with standard search engines. For most researchers, the invisible Web is a practice-makes-perfect mechanism. As you use it your skills will improve and you will experience higher quality results. It appears likely that the invisible Web will soon expand to include content from areas such as video, radio, TV broadcasts, and other types of emerging new media.

It is my belief that acquiring the expertise to effectively search the invisible Web is one of the most important skills you will learn from this book.

CHAPTER 4:
THE U.S. GOVERNMENT AND THE WEB

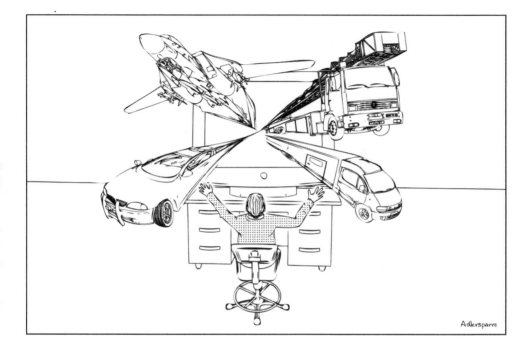

Adlersparre

In the realm of invisible Web resources, several stand out in their ability to be both useful and informative. As we all know, there are many sites that offer loads of information, but are unorganized and hard to use. There is hope, however, and from an unlikely source. Some of the most overlooked and seldom used sites on the Web are the sites of the United States Government.

Though the famous social commentator Will Rogers once stated, "Thank God we don't get all of the Government we are paying for," with the United States Government's Web based resources, this does not ring true. At the Federal level, the US Government has compiled an excellent set of resources that are largely invisible Web based and any individual with an Internet connection easily acquire them. This in-depth data covers almost every category of interest, ranging across such topics as agriculture, health, economics, and even zoology.

Unfortunately, the United States Government has not chosen to actively advertise this highly useful resource to the public. This lack of knowledge of United States Government resources is so common among the average Internet user that many of those who I have interviewed did not even know of any Government presence on the Web at all. Very few surfers or researchers knew the width and depth of the resources that are available through the Government, and some even scoffed at the idea that Government could do anything on the Web that was useful at all. Those who did know about the Government's Web presence were often unsure how best to use the resources.

The Government, by putting a large majority of its available information on the Web, is attempting to create an environment where citizens can get Government services on-demand. By offering these diverse services on the Web, the Government can improve the quality of services available, while also cutting the cost of their delivery to citizens.

United States Government information is primarily available through the www.usa.gov Website, labeled as the "US Government's Official Web Portal." Though other methods of searching for US Government data exist on the Web, www.usa.gov is both the most comprehensive and the easiest to use. The site is chock full of useful information and links, and the quality of the information rivals the content of pay-based commercial Websites. The United States Government has also decided to use the unique clustering technology provided by www.clusty.com to show the sub-categories of a search, making searching on its Websites even easier.

Upon examination of the www.usa.gov site's opening page, users encounter tabs for different versions of www.usa.gov. One each exists for citizens (most of the potential users), businesses, NGOs, non-profits, federal employees and inter-Governmental users. Once a tab is chosen, there are links to Government information by category on topics grouped according to the relevant user base. On the citizens' sector for instance, topics include such popularly relevant subjects as consumer guides, taxes, health etc.

On the left side of the opening page of the www.usa.gov site there is an A-Z list of Government agencies, links to state and local Government data, and a link to tribal Indian Government sites. Near the top of the www.usa.gov site are links to various useful services such as auctions, Government job applications, passport application procedures, etc. In addition, on the lower left of the home page, users can access links that allow them to contact the Government and get free E-mails and RSS feeds from www.usa.gov. The usa.gov search, which is located the upper right corner of the usa.gov opening page, offers both an image search and a news search. The image search of the usa.gov site offers a wide range of graphics, including images from special U.S. Government collections such as NASA, the White House, the National Park Service, etc. Most of the images in these collections are in the public domain and freely available for use.

The news search portion of the www.usa.gov site is updated every 15 minutes and groups together news from hundreds of federal agencies, offices and state Governments. As with the main Website, the news search uses the CLUSTY clustering technology to group recent stories into topics that reflect the day's most important events. Through the search area of www.usa.gov you can isolate your search to Government Web, images or news without opening a separate advanced search page. In addition to these excellent features, www.usa.gov has a reference center with links to popular search categories such as data and statistics, forms, laws and regulation, Government libraries, photos and multimedia. These links are extremely helpful to researchers who utilize Government information.

Many interesting and unusual searches can be conducted through the www.usa.gov site. I have found data on this site when it seemed impossible to find it anywhere else on the Web. Recently I tested the ability of the www.usa.gov site to come up with obscure data, by inputting the search term "sex life of a rat." The www.usa.gov Website came up with 96 hits that included facts on rat reproduction, out of 7,642 possibilities. This particular search may not be of interest to most users (assuming you are not an exterminator), but it illustrates the capability of the www.usa.gov Website to achieve results on difficult searches. The usa.gov Web search itself is powered by MSN search, and that, along with the CLUSTY technology comes up with effective search results. Though I hate to contradict Will Rogers, with the www.usa.gov Website you do get all of the Government you are paying for, and then some.

Besides www.usa.gov, there are several other search engines that search for Government information. The first of these is www.fedworld.gov, a page maintained by the U.S. Department of Commerce. In plain English, www.fedworld.gov is www.usa.gov "lite." Links on the Fed World page enable users to search for a Federal Government job, search Government research, and search for Development Publications (www.ntis.gov). It also has the ability to search www.usa.gov, U.S. Supreme Court decisions, top Government Websites, key Government science and technology Websites, and the Internal Revenue Service. Based on this information, I see no reason that anyone would choose to use this site over www.usa.gov.

Google U.S. Government search, located at www.google. com/ig/usgov, is another Government search engine. This site, a division of Google, searches solely for U.S. Government information, and is superior to its basic Google search counterpart. On the left side of each page there is weather information for Washington D.C. and American Forces Information Services notices. In the center of the page is "White House News" and the "Government Executive." On the right side of the page there is Google news, Government stories, and links to the Washington Post. On the top of the page there is a search bar which offers the option of searching Government sites, or the Web. When I used this site, I found the results of my searches to be more than acceptable, and it provides an easier to use, though less detailed, alternative to www.usa.gov.

The third Government search engine to investigate is www. searchgov.com. This interesting site is replete with useful links related to the United States Government. Directly underneath the search bar there are links to such items as the House of Representatives, the Senate, NASA, the Library of Congress, OSHA, the FAA, and other Governmental agencies. In the middle of the page, there are additional links to executive agencies and independent agencies. Below this there are links to state and local Governments in alphabetical order. This site is also interesting, but it is not as useful as www.usa.gov.

This next section will save you many hours of investigation, as it is a review of the most interesting sites and services that the Government offers over the Web. This is NOT in any way, a complete list, but rather, it is a group of sites and services that I feel are representative of the colossal amount of information that is offered by the United States Government.

THE U.S. GOVERNMENT'S MOST INTERESTING SITES & SERVICES

1. The White House, www.whitehouse.gov

This site is the link to the White House and the Executive Branch of Government. (Many users have made the unfortunate mistake of typing in www.whitehouse.com, and have found themselves at an adult oriented site. Do not make this mistake.) The White House site has a multitude of useful links to functions that are the province of the executive branch of Government, including education, homeland security, immigration, jobs, the economy, Medicare, and other useful topics. This site also allows users to listen and see major speeches and press briefings from the White House, and even allows interaction with the White House in the "Ask the White House" section. The site is logically laid out, and updated consistently with topics that are of concern to the citizens of the United States. **Rating=3**

2. The Central Intelligence Agency (CIA), www.cia.gov

There are at least two vital links that are available through this site. The first link, on the left side of the page, is to the CIA World Fact Book. This fact book is a well known, comprehensive source of unclassified data on nearly every nation and territory in the world. I have personally found this source to be of great use to both myself and to students researching data about other countries. The other interesting and vital link is to the "Fact Book on Intelligence," which shows in detail the functions of the CIA. **Rating=3.5**

3. The Federal Bureau of Investigation (FBI), www.fbi.gov

This is a really fascinating site, which includes a multitude of interesting investigations on both current and past FBI data and cases. Through this site it is possible to see the "Top Ten Most Wanted" list, which used to be available only on Post Office walls. The site also has tips on being crime smart, and the investigative priorities of the FBI, as well as the FBI in the News. I have found this site to be an interesting place to spend some time browsing, especially for the profiles of past cases and information on leading terrorists and criminals. **Rating=3.5**

4. The United States Internal Revenue Service, www.irs.gov

I realize that the mere mention of this site sends a chill down the spine of almost every reader of this book. However, in reality, the horror stories involving the Internal Revenue Service are much overstated. This site is actually an example of the IRS's attempt to reach out to the general public and to provide them with accurate tax information. Using this site, it is possible to download tax forms and publications, get answers to frequently asked questions, and see the most recent news regarding taxation. I have found this site to be extremely helpful in answering some of my simpler tax related questions. It is also much easier than calling and waiting on hold to get your questions answered. **Rating=4**

5. The Department of Homeland Security, www.dhs.gov

This newly created site has a wealth of information on security preparedness for United States citizens. The site covers threats from not only terrorist and criminal threats, but also hurricanes and other natural disasters. Additional sections that detail passport and airline regulations and provide travel advisories make this site a must for anyone who intends to travel abroad. **Rating=3**

6. The United States Computer Emergency Readiness Team, www.us-cert.gov

This site coordinates responses to and defense against cyber attacks across the nation. Among the direct links on the site are security alerts and bulletins that describe vulnerabilities in computer programs and current activity in the security area. The E-mail alert portion of this site is especially valuable, since the Government will E-mail you when a major threat occurs. **Rating=3.5**

7. The United States Department of Justice, www.justice.gov

This site details the activities of the Department of Justice, providing descriptions of current investigations and links to much requested information, such as seized assets, sales and auctions, and the Federal Inmate Locator. **Rating=3.5**

8. Social Security Online, www.ssa.gov

This site is full of pertinent information on social security and other information that is of interest to senior citizens. Using this site, it is possible to plan your retirement, calculate your retirement benefits and apply for benefits. There are also sections on Medicare, Disability and SSI, widowers and other survivors, and how to get help in the event of unusual situations, such as marriage, divorce, or death. **Rating=4**

9. Fedstats, the official gateway to Governmental statistics from over 100 U.S. Federal agencies, www.fedstats.gov

It appears that the *raison d'etre* of the U.S. Government is to collect as much information as possible, so that they can generate wonderful statistics on all of the data collected! This site is the central portal to all of these statistics. On the left side of the site's opening page, there are links that provide direct access to groups of statistical data alphabetized by topic. Below that is the link to Mapstats, which are statistical profiles of states, cities, and counties, searchable by state. Below Mapstats are geographical statistics from U.S. agencies, which have geographical data compiled from international, national, state and local community input.

Next is the Statistical Reference Shelf. This extremely useful collection of statistics includes the comprehensive statistical abstract of the United States. Under the Statistical Reference Shelf, there is a search that allows searches across agency Websites. On the right side of the Fedstats Website, there are links to even more statistical agencies. These agencies are listed alphabetically, with descriptions of the statistics that they provide and links to their Websites, contact information, and key statistics.

Following this is another list of agencies by subject, where you may select a subject from a drop down list. Along with this information are press releases from individual agencies, kids pages from agency Websites, and data access tools from selected agency online databases. Fedstats also includes additional links to other statistical sites and Federal statistical policy links (for those of you who cannot get enough of those exciting statistics!).

In summary, Fedstats is a must have for any serious searcher who needs statistical data in any area that is under the realm of the United States Government. **Rating=5**

10. Stat-USA/Internet, www.stat-usa.gov

Stat-usa/Internet is a service of the United States Department of Commerce. This site is a single point of access to authoritative business, trade and economic information from across the Federal Government. Among the links at this site, are financial releases and economic data, under the heading "State of the Nation." Another important link on this site is to Globes and the NTDB (the National Trade Data Bank). This linked area allows access to international market research, trade opportunities, trade libraries and country analysis.

To gain access to both of these sites, you have to subscribe and pay a fee of $200 annually. Despite its fee, this site provides aggregation services that may be worth the price of subscription if you do not want to travel to each individual site to cull bits of data. **Rating=3.5**

11. The Census Bureau, www.census.gov

This important site is one of the pillars of Government based information. Many other commercial and non commercial sites use data generated from this site. The breadth and depth of the data available here is extraordinary and extremely useful in any type of demographic study.

On the left side of this site, there are several links. One of them leads to American Fact Finder, which provides some of the most valuable data available on the site. On the left side of American Fact Finder, there are links to a Population Finder, with a U.S. Population clock. Below the population finder is a the Fact Sheet, which allows you to get city, town, county, or zip code information, as well as population, housing, economic and geographic data. There is also a street address search that allows one to investigate micro data from the 2000 census. The value of this data cannot be understated, or undervalued.

Additionally, there are links to people, housing, business and Government data that can be highly useful for determining the demographics of a new housing or business location.

The Business and Government section of the Census site includes two very interesting databases: the 2004 Zip Code Business Data Service, and the 2002 Economic Census, which profiles the U.S. economy every five years. (This data should be updated in 2009.) Directly below this section is a link to geography, which has maps, and the U.S. Gazetteer, a fascinating database that allows you to download the 2000 Census data for places, counties, and zip code areas. In addition, the Census Bureau has an excellent news room with links to current releases and facts, as well as broadcast and photo service. **Rating=5**

12. Your Benefits Connection, www.govbenefits.gov

This obscure but useful site provides a wealth of information on Government benefits. On this site you may fill out a questionnaire and find a complete list of programs that might provide you benefits based on your demographic information. The site also features a drop down menu of selected tragic life events, such as the sudden death of a household head, that may qualify you for Government benefits. This site will assist you with determining what you are entitled to and where to get it.

Below this, there is another drop down menu that lists the most popular benefits that the Government offers. In addition, there is a link that allows you to locate benefits in a list of state benefits programs. Another subheading leads you to a link to federal programs that allow you to search and to locate federal benefits. The site also has keyword search capability and gives search tips so that your search can be conducted efficiently. This site is extremely useful during those trying times when one may need outside assistance. **Rating=3**

13. The Gateway to Federal Loan Information, www.govloans.gov

This site, which is linked to www.govbenefits.gov, allows you to browse all available loans by keyword or to search a list of popular available loans. Among the types of loans available are: Agriculture, Business, Disaster Relief, Education, Housing and Veteran. This site, in my opinion, is especially useful when used in conjunction with other Government sites that are related to the loans that you are applying for. For instance, visit this site in tandem with www.sba.gov if you are applying for a small business loan. **Rating=3.5**

14. GovSales, the official site for the purchase of new, seized, and surplus merchandise and real estate from the Government, www.govsales.gov

The information provided by this site is among the most requested because of the allure of buying valuable items for pennies on the dollar. There is a vast amount of misconception and "folklore" regarding Government auctions and sales of property. Everyone has probably heard folk tales about people buying confiscated Porsches and Rolls Royce's for $100.00, or real estate for almost nothing. As ridiculous as this all sounds, there is still a tremendous demand for this information, provided at the www.govsales.gov site.

On the top of the site, there is a list of material that is sold or auctioned by the United States Government. Among the categories listed are: Houses, Land and Buildings, Farms, Vehicles and Parts, Aviation and Marine, Computers, Electronics, Office, Clothing and Personal, Household Goods, Industrial, Jewelry and Collectibles, Sporting Goods, and Books and Music. Certainly, there are some good buys to be had on the site and it could be worth readers' time to examine and to potentially bid on some of the available material. The reality is that there is competitive bidding for these assets and they sell at "reasonable discounts." Who knows? Maybe one day you can own the Ferrari, at a great price, that was driven by an infamous criminal... **Rating=3.5**

15. The U.S. Bureau of Labor/Bureau of Labor Statistics, www.bls.gov and stats.bls.gov

Of the myriad Government sites that we will be reviewing in this book, this may be one of the most useful and important. On this site are links to databases covering a plethora of material. I am, therefore, only commenting on what I consider to be the site's most important links. It would certainly behoove any user of the site to spend time investigating those things they find most pertinent.

Starting at the left side of the site, there is a section covering inflation and consumer spending. Among the more interesting links associated with this section are the CPI (Consumer Price Index) and PPI (Producer Price Index). A separate link to the Inflation calculator allows users to determine today's equivalent of past monetary amounts. For example, you can compare the value of $100.00 today with the value of $100.00 back in 1963.

Below this there are sections related to Wages, Earnings, and Benefits, all of which feature subsections to delineate these topics by area, occupation and industry. Another section, Productivity, covers productivity and costs, multi-factor productivity, and international comparisons. The next important category is International, which includes import, and export price indices and foreign labor statistics. Also included is a category entitled Demographics, which provides links to the demographic characteristics of the labor force, the geographic profile of employment and unemployment, and consumer expenditures.

The last category featured on the site's left hand side is Occupations, which includes two of the most important publications that are distributed by the Government. The first one is the "Occupational Outlook Handbook," which states the current and future prospects for employment by category. This is a particularly valuable resource for high school and college students entering the workforce for the first time. The second is the "Occupational Outlook Quarterly," which describes quarterly changes in the data covered by the Handbook. Another important part of the site lists wages by area and occupation to enable users to determine if they are being paid within the typical salary parameters of their industry.

In the center of the site is a synopsis of the latest numbers for important economic indicators, such as the CPI, the PPI, the unemployment rate, productivity rate, and other indicators of our nation's economic health. A nice, user friendly touch is the little dinosaur icon to the left of these indicators. When the dinosaur is clicked, it gives ten years of historical data for that indicator. There is also a link to regional resources, where you may select either a state map or a drop-down menu for additional state information.

On the right side of the site are the categories of Employment and Unemployment. These include national employment and unemployment figures, state and local employment/unemployment, employment projections by occupation, job openings, and labor turnover.

This is an excellent resource for those who are thinking of switching positions in the near future, people who are currently unemployed, or people who are thinking of joining the labor force in a particular area of industry and want to see current demand for workers.

Next in line are the tables, showing the United States economy and industries at a glance, followed by regions, state and areas, also at a glance. Below that are additional publications of note such as the Monthly Labor Review Online, Compensations and

Working Conditions Online, and the Career Guide to Industry. In addition, there are links to research papers and industrial data.

A final interesting section is Geography, which has state and local profiles of employment and unemployment and rates and wages. An interesting feature of this section is the ability to create customized maps. Based upon the enormous amount of information available here, and the fact that many other sites draw data from this site as well, I highly recommend this site as an addition to any serious researcher's favorites list. **Rating=4.5**

16. The Official Business Link to the U.S. Government, www.business.gov

As a small business owner and professor of business, I have noted that there is a tremendous amount of data available for free from the United States Government that can be extremely helpful for business purposes. Most business owners think of the Government as an enemy, and certainly the last place to go to for important data. In actuality, the Government may be your best friend. Unenlightened business owners may spend thousands of dollars on professionals or commercial services for similar data that is available for free through the United States Government.

On the left side of the business.gov site there is a business resource library that has links to information on regulatory topics, business licenses and permits, hiring and managing employees, taxes, etc. On the right side of the page, there is a link to federal forms that provides similar data to that given by the www.forms.gov site. Below this there is a link to compliance information on both the Federal and State levels, which can also be accessed through a search bar in the middle of the page.

Below the compliance section, there is a link to SBA that provides information on how to start, finance, and manage a small business. Close to this is a link to small business resources. You may search the whole site by industry or business topic, investigating subjects like business law, finance, information security and non-profits. This is coupled with information pertaining to most of the common industries such as energy, health care, mining, transportation, etc. **Rating=4**

17. The United States Small Business Administration, www.sba.gov

This site is loaded with a wealth of helpful information for the small business owner. Among the resources available are: how to start, finance, and manage a small business, and a library of useful information for small businesses. The examination and use of this site is mandatory for the students enrolled in my small business classes. There are many forms available through the site that can be used by small business owners. Through the SBA site, the U.S. Government also helps small businesses learn how to write effective business plans, and comply with small business laws and regulations. Unfortunately, most small business owners have little if any idea of how to comply with laws and regulations that pertain to their particular small business. There are many forms available through the site that can be used by small business owners. It is also possible for a small business owner to subscribe to informational news letters that are distributed by the SBA for free. Furthermore, SBA has a small business online chat on several topics hosted by industry experts. On the right side of the site there are links to top news stories that pertain to small business. This site is extremely helpful to a small business owner, especially when starting up a new venture. **Rating=4.5**

18. The Federal Trade Commission, www.ftc.gov

The Federal Trade Commission (FTC) performs an extremely important function in the lives of both consumers and businesses. The FTC is an advocate for both consumers and businesses against unfair business practices and unscrupulous behavior, such as false advertising, unsubstantiated claims and identity theft. Among the benefits of this Website is the ability to file a complaint against a business for deceptive practices through the site. This is a great improvement over the old system of calling or mailing a complaint to the local Better Business Bureau or the Department of Consumer Affairs, filing a form, and waiting for your complaint to be processed. The FTC site also hosts the National Do Not Call Registry and On Guard Online, a safety net against cyber fraud. The FTC has a huge task before it in protecting consumers and businesses from unscrupulous behavior, including such false and predatory practices as: Bait and Switch, false and unsubstantiated advertising, unsubstantiated claims, and identity theft. In addition, the Federal Trade Commission controls fair credit practices for consumers and hosts the Free Annual Credit report site (the only truly free site for credit reports), as a link.

Under consumer information, the FTC has links to such important categories as automobiles, credit, diet, health, and fitness, e-commerce, energy and the environment, franchise and business opportunities, identity theft, investments, privacy, telemarketing, telephone service, and travel. Under each category, there are additional links to consumer information in both PDF and text format that relate to problems consumers may have with goods and service. A typical article under consumer information would be: "The Nigerian Scam: Costly Compassion," which describes this scam in detail and explains how to avoid it. The breadth and depth of the information available on the FTC site is so great that mastery of this site would be helpful to any citizen. **Rating=5**

19. The U.S. Securities and Exchange Commission, www.sec.gov

This is the official site for information on stocks and other securities in the United States. This site has information for investors such as portfolio calculators, procedures for filing a tip or a complaint against a financial advisor, and past financial histories of various brokers and financial firms. In addition, the SEC disseminates news through their news digest and public press releases, as well as via Webcasts from the SEC. Another interesting section is the release of litigious and regulatory action against brokers, dealers, securities issuers and advisors.

In addition to this wealth of excellent information, the most popular portion of this site is in the EDGAR listings. EDGAR allows users to search for company filings with the U.S. Government. EDGAR is an excellent source of data for fundamental financial information filed with the SEC. It is a legal requirement that all publicly held reporting companies must file three quarterly 10Qs and one annual 10K report with the SEC in order to maintain their reporting status. These reports provide a detailed roadmap into the financial condition of the reporting companies. In addition, other forms, such as 144-Registrations (restricted stock sales) and 13D reports (purchases of 5% or more of the common stock of a public company) are also revealed on the SEC site. Use of this site is vital to any individual who owns common stock in any currently reporting company that is subject to corporate governance. **Rating=4**

20. The U.S. Financial Literacy and Education Commission, www.mymoney.gov

Mymoney.gov is the U.S. Government Website dedicated to teaching Americans the basics of financial education. As the site itself says, "Whether you're planning to buy a home, balancing your checkbook, or vesting in your 401K, the resources on mymoney.gov can help you do it better." There are many topics listed such as, budgeting and taxes, credit, home ownership, privacy, fraud and scams, retirement planning, and savings and investing, among other useful links.

The site links to important information from twenty other Federal agencies and is a very nice basic Website for the average individual, enhancing their knowledge of how to use their money more effectively. **Rating=3**

21. The Commodity Futures Trading Commission, www.cftc.gov

This site describes the regulations and operations of the U.S. Commodity Exchanges. The site may be of interest to commodities traders, investors in commodities, and those individuals who monitor the prices of commodities as a part of their ordinary business. **Rating=4**

22. The Department of Commerce, www.commerce.gov

This site describes the Government's relationship with import and export businesses in the United States. It features material that would be of interest to those who conduct international trade, such as trade statistics, trade opportunities for business, and import/export related market information. **Rating=4**

23. The Department of the Treasury, www.ustreas.gov

This site links users to the functions of the Treasury Department. On the left side of the site there are links useful to money managers, businesses and investors, including information on how to purchase treasury bills (T- Bills), treasury bonds and Savings Bonds. Also included are procedures for contacting and interacting with the Treasury, and some fascinating interest rate statistics. In addition, users may also browse topics such as accounting and budget, currency and coins, the economy and financial markets. The site also links to the Treasury Direct site located at www.treasurydirect.gov. Www.treasurydirect.gov enables you to purchase electronic securities directly from the Treasury, set up and manage accounts, and obtain information about treasury securities that you already own. **Rating=3.5**

24. The United States Patent and Trademark Office, www.uspto.gov or patents.uspto.gov.

Under current U.S. patent, trademark, and copyright law, all current patents, trademarks, and copyrights must be available to the general public for examination. This site is a clearinghouse that gives descriptions of the current patents, trademarks, and copyrights in the database. In addition, the site shows how to apply for a patent, trademark, or copyright. **Rating=4**

25. The U.S. Department of Energy, www.doe.gov

This site has an abundance of facts on energy, the environment, energy efficiency, prices, and trends. There are links to energy saving devices and renewable energy sources. There is also a search mechanism located on the upper right hand side of the site that allows users to find a vast amount of information on the subject of energy. This site also links to a sister site at www.fueleconomy.gov, which provides information about gasoline prices, hybrid vehicles, energy efficiency, and a side by side comparison of information for new and used cars and trucks. **Rating=4**

26. The U.S. Environmental Protection Agency, Enviromapper for Super Fund, www.epa.gov/enviro/sf

This tool combines interactive maps and aerial photography to map, display, and query sites by zip code, city, county and state. Via this site a prospective homebuyer or other property purchaser may enter in their zip code and find out exactly what, if any, environmental hazards exist in the area. **Rating=4.5**

27. The National Aeronautics and Space Administration, www.nasa.gov

As an Internet researcher I have found that man cannot live by data alone. This beautiful site, and sites associated with it, covers the journey of man in space. In the main site, www.nasa.gov, a user may investigate space shuttle and space station programs, watch NASA exploration videos and explore the constellation program.

Another page linked to the NASA site, http://hubble.nasa.gov, is home to the Hubble Space Telescope, the legendary vehicle of astronomic exploration that has produced some of the most breathtaking images of our universe. This site not only describes the history and operation of the telescope, but also gives links to the pictures taken by the Hubble telescope.

An excellent site linked to the NASA site is the Planetary Photo Journal at http://photojournal.jpl.nasa.gov. This site allows users to explore the planets in great detail, and investigate various stars and small interstellar bodies.

Another wonderful and relatively unknown site is the Whirlwind Project at http://whirlwind.arc.nasa.gov. This free download (a large program) lets you zoom from satellite altitude to any point of the face of the earth. Whirlwind lets you experience terrain in visually rich 3D, as if you were really there. Using Whirlwind, you may visit just about any place in the world. Whirlwind appears to be the premiere satellite imaging service with picture quality exceeding that of other popular competing services. **Rating=5**

28. The U.S. Department of the Interior, www.doi.gov

This site is notable for its beautiful pictures of national parks. DOI has placed Webcams in many national parks to allow visitor observation of such sights as the Old Faithful Glacier, the Grand Canyon, Mammoth Hot Springs, and Big Ben National Park. It can be quite entertaining to tune in to the Webcams and watch Old Faithful go off, or watch a buffalo stroll through Yellowstone National Park in real time. In addition to these lovely Webcams, the site has many interesting facts on the role of the DOI in national conservation and protection. There are links on this site to wildlife, adoption and conservation, and a list of endangered species. There are also maps to all of the national parks listed. **Rating=3.5**

29. The Government Printing Office Access, www.gpoaccess.gov

The U.S. Government Printing Office disseminates official information from all three branches of the Federal Government. Primarily, this site links to some of the pay resources, such as special booklets and documentation that the Government sells to customers in the U.S. Government Online Bookstore, but also has many links to free resources offered by the Legislative, Executive and Judicial branches of Government. **Rating=3**

30. The United States Postal Service, www.usps.com

This is one of the few Government sites in the dot com domain, and is quite familiar to Internet users. This site has links to zip code indices, postage calculation procedures, shipping label printing, post office locations, pickup schedules and tracking and delivery confirmation of packages. In addition, this site provides information on change of address procedure, post office box rentals, and mail holds. This site is extremely user friendly and may be one of the most useful Government sites for individuals and small businesses who frequently use the post office. **Rating=4**

31. The Federal Forms Catalog for Citizens, www.forms.gov

This site provides citizens and businesses with an access point to Federal agency forms. On the left side are links to the most frequently used forms such as tax forms, small business forms, Veteran's Benefits forms, SSI forms, and FEMA forms.

On the main portion of this site is a search mechanism that allows you to locate a form by keyword or form number. Below this is a portal that allows for searches by agency or sub-agency from A to Z, and by form name from A to Z. This relatively unknown U.S. Government site offers a tremendous convenience, as it can often be time consuming to get Government forms mailed to you. **Rating=4.5**

32. The Federal Citizen Information Center, www.pueblo.gsa.gov

This site provides links to many free Government publications on topics such as, cars, grants, home purchasing and credit.

The site is very easy to use, and produces excellent results when searched. **Rating=4.5**

33. The Federal Government's Official Jobs, www.usajobs.gov

One of the questions that I field most from college students is, "How do I find a job with the U.S. Government?" This site is the central, one stop source for federal jobs and employment information. Within the site the job searcher first creates a résumé and stores it. The job searcher then states which jobs he or she is looking for and the desired geographical location. Once there is a match, USA Jobs will send an E-mail notifying you to apply for the job.

In addition, there is a large database that has a list of all the Federal jobs that are currently available and the requirements for each job. This is an excellent resource for any individual who would like to start a career with the United States Government. **Rating=4**

34. Government Grants, www.grants.gov

The U.S. Government offers billions of dollars in Federal grants. This site allows users to find and apply for any grants that may be of interest. **Rating=3.5**

35. The Consumer Action, www.consumeraction.gov

The consumer action page is notable because it allows a user to sign up for the "Consumer Action Handbook." This everyday guide to smart shopping is full of helpful hints regarding identity theft, understanding credit, buying a car or a home, digital television, etc.

All of the information in the printed edition of the Consumer Action Handbook is also available on this site. On the right hand side are other links to recent consumer hot topics and featured material. **Rating=4**

36. Your Online Resource for Recalls, www.recalls.gov

This site is the simpler version of the Consumer Products Safety Commission site (fwww.cpsc.gov). Www.recalls.gov describes products that may have been recalled, like motor vehicles, boats, food, consumer products, medicines, cosmetics, and environmental products. On the left side of the page, there are links to recent recalls, a search platform to find recalls, E-mail recall alert registration, and *Informacion en espanol*. You can also learn important safety tips or report a dangerous product.

The main site for information on dangerous and defective products is the U.S. Consumer Product Safety Council, at www.cpsc.gov. However, unless you need in depth information on defective products, the www.recalls.gov site should be sufficient. **Rating=4**

37. The Center for Disease Control and Prevention, www.cdc.gov

This site explains potential health risks and offers a wide variety of information related to health and safety. On the left side of the site, there are links to topics, such as Diseases and Conditions, Environmental Health, Vaccines and Immunizations, and Traveler's Health.

Below this there is a link to publications and products related to health, including an RSS feed from this site. Further below these are data and statistics that are related to health and disease issues. In the center of the site, there are also links to such topics as breast cancer, genomics, pandemic flu and avian influenza (Bird Flu). As a sidenote, for those of you who are history buffs, the CDC was one of the first sites to make information available regarding HIV/AIDS. **Rating=4**

38. The United States Food and Drug Administration, www.fda.gov

This site describes the functions of the FDA and the many products that the FDA regulates. There is information for consumers, patients and health professionals. There is also an area where you may report a problem with a product that is under the FDA's jurisdiction. This site also features information on current FDA affairs such as imported drugs and the spinach E. Coli outbreak. **Rating=4**

39. The Nutrition Information, www.nutrition.gov

Many Americans are interested in having proper nutrition and maintaining a healthy diet so that they can improve their general health. Our Government is thus getting involved in nutrition issues such as Trans Fat or Childhood Obesity. Given the plethora of information available in the area of nutrition, it is nice to have a trusted site for unbiased nutritional information. There is much valuable content available here, including nutritional facts, weight management techniques, shopping strategies, as well as recipes and meal planning. It also includes the new and improved Food Pyramid.

In the center of the page, there is also a section entitled "In the News," which spotlights "hot" topics in the nutritional arena. Some examples are the new fruit and vegetable calorie calculator, a nationwide study on the effects of anti-oxidants, and sugar quantities in your favorite food. Considering the health consciousness of many people today, this is certain to remain a useful and informative site. **Rating=4**

40. Food Safety Information, www.foodsafety.gov

This is the gateway to Government food safety information. On the left side of the start page, there are sections on news and safety alerts, consumer advice, kids, teens and educators, illness reporting, product complaints, and food borne pathogens. In the center of the page, there is "from farm to table," and below that frequently asked questions in video format. On the right side of the page there is industry assistance, national food safety programs, Federal and State Government agencies, a search, and the site index. At the bottom of the page there are selected highlights that include recent food safety issues.

This site is excellent for those consumers concerned about food recalls and the most recent food safety issues. **Rating=4**

41. Medline Plus Health Information from the National Library of Medicine, www.medlineplus.com

This site has links to over 700 topics on diseases, health and wellness, drugs and supplements, over the counter medicines, and herbs. It also features a medical encyclopedia and dictionary, and a directory to find doctors, dentists, and hospitals.

An interesting feature is the availability of over 165 interactive tutorials on medical topics. There are also links to information on clinical trials and senior health, surgery videos, and the Medline Plus magazine. There is a wealth of information (some not for the squeamish) for the health conscious consumer. **Rating=4.5**

42. http://travel.state.gov, via the U.S. State Department

In the tumultuous world that we live in, American citizens face a variety of problems when traveling abroad often due to the socio-political conditions that exist in to the nations visited. This site seeks to address these issues, and provides links to international travel information, passport service procedures for U.S. citizens, and visa information for foreign citizens. Additional links are provided to register with embassies, stay safe while traveling abroad, and list required documents for traveling to various countries.

This site is actually the simpler version of the U.S. Department of State site at www.state.gov, which also contains a plethora of important information regarding traveling abroad. A particularly useful section provides links to travel warnings that describe, nation by nation, particular conditions that may be hazardous to U.S. travelers. These warnings can be E-mailed to users after registration with the site. The U.S. State Department site also provides links to emergency services, country background notes that describe current conditions in each of the world's nations, and passport requirements for each foreign nation. This site should be a mandated stop for any U.S. citizen traveling outside of the United States. **Rating=5**

43. The Federal Aviation Administration, www.faa.gov

The FAA site has links to airports and air traffic, airline data and statistics, and FAA travel rules (these apply only to aircraft). On the right side of the site, there are links to airport status and delays, as well as accident and incident reports from the FAA.

The most valuable aspect of this site is the FAA's continued monitoring of airlines, and ranking of the efficiency of various airlines. **Rating=4.5**

44. The U.S. Department of Transportation, www.dot.gov

This Website is notable because it allows users to receive detailed information on airlines, motor carriers, and truckers. You may address complaints regarding any licensed transportation service directly to the D.O.T. using this site. **Rating=3.5**

45. The National Traffic and Road Closure Information, www.rhwa.dot.gov/trafficinfo/index/htm

This is an almost unknown Website, even among Government employees. This wonderful site has links to almost everything traffic related on a state by state basis. It features construction information, local and state transit links, traffic conditions, regional links, and weather and road conditions.

There is also a map on the site that allows users to click on any individual state for local information. I also was impressed with the quality of the links that corresponded with national road and weather conditions. This site is indispensable to travelers seeking to avoid delays. **Rating=4**

46. The National Atlas, www.nationalatlas.gov

This site allows users to print pre-formatted maps, categorized by topic. Available mapping subjects include agriculture, biology, boundaries, climate, environment, geology, Government, history, people, and transportation. Using this site, you can even order custom larger maps suitable for the wall of your office or classroom, based on the parameters you specify. One can download all maps generated by the site at no cost and use them freely without copyright concerns or license restrictions. **Rating=4**

47. The National Map, http://nationalmap.gov

The National Map is an online interactive map service that you can view through your browser without using any special software. The National Map provides public access to accurate topographical maps derived from high quality data from multiple partners. The detail on these maps is excellent.

This is a wonderful addition for searchers who use data from better known mapping services. This map enables you to zoom in and out and designate other custom features. **Rating=4**

48. Recreation Maps, www.recreationmaps.gov

This obscure site allows users to find maps based on area name within a range or radius of a particular location. For instance, you may find a map for recreational areas within 25 miles of Denver, Colorado, or maps based on activity and state. **Rating=4**

49. Ben's Guide to U.S. Government for Kids, http://bensguide.gpo.gov

This site has information for children in grade levels K to 12, as well as for parents and teachers. It simplifies the complexities of the Government so that youngsters can understand how the Government works. The site is user friendly, easy to read and understand, and can make studying Government seem "cool" to youngsters. **Rating=4**

50. The Library of Congress, www.loc.gov

This is the single largest site in the world, and the front page barely conveys the sheer complexity and depth of the data contained within. On top are links to the library catalogues; print, multi media, and online resources; American Memory (a collection of historic maps, photos, documents, audio, and video); Exhibitions in the Library (containing treasures from these collections); Global Gateway on World Culture; and THOMAS, which is the gateway to current and historical legislative information. Below this there are highlights from the Library's news and events.

There is a wide variety of other search tools and informative components to the Website. The Library of Congress online catalogue allows for basic search, guided search, and search by type. There is a program called Library Thing, available at www. librarything.com, that allows you to catalogue books online by searching Amazon.com, the Library of Congress, and sixty other sources around the world. One can conduct their search by title, author, ISBN number and several other methods. Once these books are added to the Librarything catalogue, a searcher can recall them on demand. Librarything allows up to 100 books to be catalogued for free, and permits users to purchase higher storage capacity.

The American Memory section of the Library of Congress site allows users to browse the Library of Congress' collections by topic. Among the topics covered are: advertising, African American history, cities and towns, Government and law, maps, presidents, technology and industry, and war and military. To illustrate the depth of the data available, I am going to highlight two of the Library's collections and describe them in detail.

The Map Collection, which holds only a small fraction of the over 4.5 millions maps that the Library of Congress owns, is a vital educational site. The maps contained here have been converted to digital format and are not covered by copyright protection. They can, therefore, be freely used. The Map collections are broken into topics such as, cities and towns, conservation and environment, exploration and discovery, cultural landscapes, military battles and campaigns, and transportation and communication. I have found that the maps available from the Library of Congress are both striking and informative.

The Law Library of Congress collection is a digital law library that features research services such as the Law Library Reading Room, digital resources such as the Guide to Law Online, and general information about the Law Library.

The next noteworthy area on the Library of Congress site is the Exhibition Section. This may be the most interesting part of the entire Library of Congress site. Many informative graphical exhibits are featured such as: "Bound for Glory: America in Color, 1939-1943"; and "Enduring Outrage," editorial cartoons by Herblock. Occasionally, the Library of Congress also offers old time television and radio broadcasts that are of historical interest to the nation.

Global Gateway is the Library of Congress' depository for World Culture and Resources. In this section are collaborative digital libraries built with international partners, and individual digital collections. A valuable database resource located within the site is that hosted by the Centers for International Research, which provides access to the Library's twenty-one reading rooms. The reading rooms focus upon specific content such as, "featured presentations," "selected items of importance," "international exhibitions," "portals to the world" (electronic resources on the nations of the worlds), as well as research guides and databases (where you may search country studies, foreign law materials, and digitized books and journals), and "international cyber casts" available through the Cyber Library of Congress Website. This information is quite comprehensive, particularly that on nations of the world and country studies.

Our final foray into the Library of Congress Website will be Thomas, at http://thomas.loc.gov, which gives in-depth legislative information from the Library of Congress. This site is named after Thomas Jefferson, who was renowned for his intellectual curiosity and love of detail and learning. Thomas monitors the activities of the legislative and judicial branches of Government.

On the front page of Thomas, on the left hand side, you may search for the text of a bill by either words or by bill number. Directly below that, you may browse bills by sponsor in either the House or the Senate. Beneath that there are links to more legislation, including previous Congress Sessions, appropriation bills and public laws. In the bottom portion of the page, you may search for other legislative activity, such as the Congressional Record, committee reports, treaties, and other links. On the top right hand side of Thomas there is a link to current activity, including "Yesterday in Congress," "The Congressional Record," the "Latest Daily Digest," "On the House Floor Now," and "Schedules and Calendars." Beneath this are links to information about the legislative and judicial branches of the Government, as well as historical texts such as the Declaration of Independence, and the U.N. Constitution.

Directly below this there is a video that features an actor describing the history of the U.S. Government. Thomas is a valuable resource for those individuals interested in the legislative and judicial branches of Government. **Rating=5**

52. U.S. Department of Commerce, Economics and Statistics Administration, www.esa.doc.gov

This site is one of two I will recommend to replace the recently closed Economic Indicators.gov site. This new Economic and Statistics Administration site has a link to the latest economic indicators, complete with summaries. It also has a keyword information search area. In addition, there are links to the Bureau of Economic Analysis (BEA), the U.S. Census site, Stat:USA, and the U.S. Department of Commerce. On the left of the page there are links to other economic indicators, economic links, and employment statistics and reports. This site is quite useful and is recommended as a stopover for all persons interested in economic statistics. **Rating=4**

53. The Bureau of Economic Analysis, www.bea.gov

This "one stop shopping" site is replete with useful statistics on the United States economy. On the home page there are separate sections and links to U.S. Economic Accounts Data divided into National, International, Regional, and Industry categories. On the left side of the page there are links to Economic News, Publications and Resources.

There is also a very interesting area entitled "Did You Know?" which illustrates the many uses of the BEA's data. On the right side of the page there is "economic information of interest," and "latest estimates" in categories that include Gross Domestic Product, Personal Income, etc. **Rating=4.5**

In addition to all of the Federal resources covered in this book, a researcher must also know and be able to use state and local Government Websites. As discussed in the first part of this chapter, www.usa.gov has extremely comprehensive lists of state and local resources, but some have reported that they find it a bit difficult to use. The state and local Government on the Website www.statelocalgov.net has a directory of official state, county and city Government Websites. On the left side of the page, there are three drop-down menus where you may select a state, a topic, and the type of Government you are researching. In the middle of the page, there is an alphabetical list of all fifty states, possessions, commonwealths, and territories, as well as tribal Governments. On the right side of the page is a topic list of typical topics and Government type's i.e. legislative, or judicial.

55. State Master, www.statemaster.com

Although Statemaster.com is not a true U.S. Government site, it is a statistical aggregator of Government information and thus merits placement in this chapter. State Master accumulates information from various primary Government sources, including the Census bureau, the FBI, and the National Bureau of Educational Statistics. State Master provides visualizations via charts, maps, graphs and scatter plots, along with thousands of maps, flag insignia, and statistical correlations. This unique site allows users to visualize state-by-state, an array of useful information concerning their state. On the front page of State Master, there is a map of the United States, where you may click and get a state's statistics. There are also links to "top stats," "stats in the news," and recent updates through the database. State Master may be searched by "all," which searches encyclopedias, statistics and forums; or by "facts and statistics," which it searches by category. This site is highly recommended. **Rating=4.5**

Considering the vast amount of information available from the United States Government the Websites described here do a magnificent job of organizing and presenting their complex data for the benefit of everyone with an Internet connection.

Many of the citizens in the United States complain about their taxes, and how the Government, ". . . wastes their money on projects that they believe do not benefit the majority of Americans." This chapter proves that the Government is in fact spending our tax money to benefit the greater good, by allowing U.S. citizens free access to a world of useful information. It is a modern example of both participatory Government and indirect democracy within our country.

CHAPTER 5:
BROWSERS AND SEARCH ENGINES ON THE INTERNET

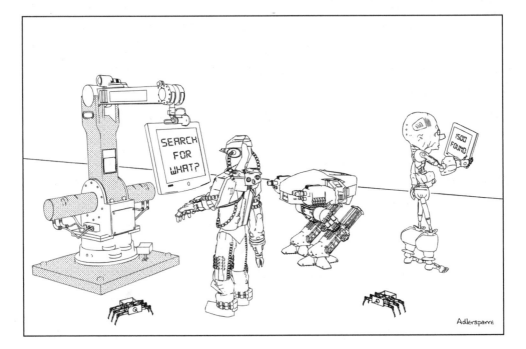

E ver since the inception of the Internet in the early 1990s there have been browsers and search engines available. A Web browser is like a telephone that can "call up" hundreds or thousands of Websites. These sites are like phone numbers listed in a massive and detailed telephone directory. However, the directory is so vast that we need a directory assistance operator in order to use it. In computer terms, that "operator" is a search engine.

Early search mechanisms such as Archie, Veronica and Jughead have evolved into modern search browsers, like Internet Explorer, and search engines, like www.clusty.com. In order to achieve an effective Internet search users must choose their search engines wisely. In this chapter, I will be describing the features of some of the more useful and effective browsers and search engines. I have listed a number of search engines along with their strengths and weaknesses in the hope that this will improve your searching capabilities. Additionally, I have listed many of the more popular browsers along with their individual strengths and weaknesses so readers can choose the browser that best meets their needs.

BROWSERS AVAILABLE ON THE INTERNET

1. Internet Explorer, www.microsoft.com

In earlier days of the Internet, Netscape was the browser of choice. In today's Internet, the browser Internet Explorer (IE) is now the most widely used, and recently issued its newest incarnation, as of this writing, IE7. Internet Explorer has been the king of Internet browsers for a long time, and like many long serving Kings, it has many problems and weaknesses. For example, IE comes packaged with Windows and is thus usually the first and only browser users will encounter, unless they do additional research to find other browsers that may be equivalent or superior.

In its favor, IE7 is easy to use and is compatible with most toolbars (these will be reviewed in a later chapter). IE7 also has a useful interface which makes it easy to get to Websites and to print and conduct other functions. Additionally, it has a redesigned interface, tabbed browsing, a built in RSS, a feed reader, a new Favorites center and optional features such as anti-phishing and malware protection.

Other problems and weaknesses for the new IE7 release include a need to run Windows XP release 2 in order to install this browser. This makes it difficult to get IE7 on many of the older legacy machines. IE is also slow at times and is a problem for older or low memory machines. In addition, the redesigned tool-bar in IE7 seems crowded and hard to use. However, the biggest and most troublesome issue is the proliferation of security prob-lems. It seems that a week does not go by without the need for a patch or some other announcement regarding another IE security problem. Most of the people I know who are serious Internet users tend to use other browsers instead of IE due to the recur-ring security concerns associated with it. Lastly, as of this writ-ing there have been several reported compatibility problems with certain programs and IE7 which may cause serious problems for some users. These problems will likely be addressed and cor-rected quickly, but some compatibility issues may remain for a while. Considering the fact that many other Microsoft programs, such as Word, integrate with IE you MUST keep IE on your sys-tem whether you intend to use it or not. Due to this practice of bundling IE with the Windows operating system, IE will likely remain the most widely used and popular browser for Windows based computers. **Rating=2**

2. Maxthon, www.maxthon.com

This IE look-alike is an extremely popular alternative to IE for many of the more knowledgeable users of the Internet. Maxthon is a tabbed browser that has the look and feel of IE, making the changeover relatively simple. Additionally, Maxthon has privacy protection that allows you to delete your Internet viewing history either automatically at exit, or whenever you request a clearing of the site history. Maxthon also includes an ad hunter that allows you to both auto filter and selectively get rid of ads and pop-ups. There is also a feature that reads RSS feeds and supports most IE compatible plug-ins. Maxthon also recently introduced a pro-gram called Maxthon Access, which is a free service that allows remote access to your home or office computer via the Maxthon browser. Most importantly, however, Maxthon uses about 65% fewer resources than IE and seems extremely stable in comparison. I myself use Maxthon often and believe it is an excellent alternative to IE for those who want IE compatibility without IE's inherent problems. Unfortunately, Maxthon does not seem to be compatible with many of the toolbars available for IE, such as Alexa and Amazon's A9. **Rating=4**

3. Avant Browser, www.avantbrowser.com

This is another IE look-alike that is very popular among Internet users. It is also very similar in look and function to Maxthon, and fully IE compatible.

In addition, Avant browser has a flash animation filter, a built in ad/pop-up blocker, and an RSS reader. In addition, the Avant browser has a full screen mode, multi-window browsing capability, and privacy controls. Performance-wise it is very stable, uses little memory and has few security holes. There is not a tremendous amount of difference between the Avant browser and Maxthon so the one that you like best should be your browser of choice. **Rating=4.5**

4. Firefox 3.0, www.mozilla.com

This increasingly popular alternative browser to IE has been around for a while but has just recently received the recognition it deserves. Firefox has a very different look and feel than IE and IE counterparts like Maxthon. The new release of this popular browser has some interesting features including improved tabbed browsing and a built-in spell checker.

Some of the search engines in Firefox 3 can suggest terms based on your search (this works with Google, Yahoo and Answers.com) by using the integrated search bar. This browser's bar comes preloaded with Google, Amazon, eBay, Answers.com and other common search engines. There is also a session restore feature which picks up a session where it was left off. In addition, Firefox has a useful feature called "live bookmarks" that lets users view Web feeds, such as news and blog headlines, in the bookmarks toolbar or menu. Lastly, Firefox has an integrated pop-up blocker. With its most recent release Firefox has become an excellent and popular alternative to IE and a top flight browser in its own right. **Rating=4**

5. Opera 9, www.opera.com

Until recently this browser was available in two versions; either a pay option or a free version that was loaded with obtrusive ads. Opera looks and acts differently then its alternatives, IE or Firefox, and can be used in either an image-rich, java-based format, or a plain non java-based format. Opera is a fast, secure alternative to other browsers, and features built-in 128 bit encryption and enhanced security for online transactions.

Opera has several other interesting features, such as a configurable content blocker and a site preference feature (that allows users to determine cookie and pop-up settings on a site-to-site basis), a feature that allows you to incorporate your favorite search engines, thumbnail preview capability, and the ability to add small multimedia applications ("widgets"). Opera also has tabbed browsing, a password manager and a fast forward feature that will try to detect the next link a user is likely to try.

In addition, Opera has the ability to place notes on a Web page and it has the unique capability of a voice feature that allows you to control the browser with your voice and instruct it to read documents out loud. This is a great feature, and especially valuable for the sight impaired user.

Opera also has a strong private data deletion mode and built in mail RSS and IRC chat capability, as well as an info panel that shows details of the page being viewed. Pound for pound Opera has the most features of any browser, though it does take some getting used to and does not have the capability to use add-ons often featured in other browsers. **Rating=4**

6. AOL Explorer, www.aol.com

This browser is IE compatible and can be downloaded as a stand-alone browser or with AOL Instant Messaging. It supports tabbed browsing and was one of the first browsers to use thumbnail previews of Web pages in various parts of AOL Explorer.

AOL Explorer also includes desktop widgets that allow users to open AOL as a side panel and use it separately from the core browser even once you close the AOL Explorer. AOL Explorer also has a feeds screensaver that displays RSS feeds stored in the feeds panel as a screensaver. AOL Explorer is not a widely used browser and most Internet users do not use it as their default browser. **Rating=2**

7. Flock, www.flock.com

This unusual and lesser known browser is Mozilla based and integrates the sharing of photos, favorites, blogging, and news items into the browser's interface. Flock supports such popular services as Flickr, Wordpress, Blogger, and others, as well as any RSS feed you choose. Flock also includes drag and drop sharing of photos, and a good Web search toolbar. Flock is a good browser choice if a user wants to do photo sharing or blog from directly within a browser. **Rating=2.5**

Search Engines

Once the Internet user chooses a browser, they must then decide which search engine will produce them the best results with the least amount of time and effort. There are a myriad of search engines, and though many of them are obscure they can still be of use to many Internet users. In the prior chapters I discussed some of these browsers, but in this section I will compare and contrast a representative group, including those browsers that are, in my opinion, the best to use for an efficient search. This is also only a small sample of what a typical user can find on the Internet. They are not listed in any particular rank or order.

1. Google, www.google.com

This search engine is so common that it has entered the English language; "Google" is actually a verb that means "search on the Web." It is also, unfortunately, somewhat of an anachronism: a set of useful and ground-breaking tools combined with a poor search engine. Google is akin to a beautiful new luxury car with the engine of a 1948 DeSoto. I will describe the tools that are available as part of Google's offerings in a later chapter, but as a search engine Google is run-of-the-mill and produces unremarkable results. As a general rule, a search on Google, while very fast, produces a tremendous amount of results, many of which are off-topic or are ad-sponsored links that pay for search engine placement. Google lacks invisible Web capability and does not rank by confidence, or utilize result clustering, or meta-search capability. Until Google improves it will rank as a poor choice of a search engine for the informed, savvy researcher. **Rating=1**

2. Yahoo, www.yahoo.com

In the past Yahoo was the best search engine on the Internet and a pioneer in the use of user-submitted and indexed material for searching. Recently, Yahoo has become much like Google, an average, general search engine combined with a few useful tools. A typical Yahoo search provides the similar problematic results of a typical Google search, but seems slightly better. Until there is significant improvement, I feel that Yahoo will remain a popular search engine that usually yields poor search results. **Rating=2**

3. Surfwax, www.surfwax.com

Surfwax is a standard meta-search engine with some interesting features. These include "look ahead," which is a dynamic site search available to Website managers and available for patents and blogs from the Surfwax front page. Surfwax also includes links to an RSS feed search and news accumulator, and to a shopping search. Despite these interesting features the real research value of Surfwax is the ability to get "snaps" on any result of a search. These snaps describe the amount of links, images, words and forms in the search. Below this area is a summary of the site, areas that are matched in context to the search, key points, and site focus words that find possible word matches to terms that are associated with your search. This is a valuable tool that gets to the heart of your search, shows the relationships within your search, and makes it easy to expand search results.

Overall, Surfwax is a unique and useful search tool, provided that users recognize the limitations of its searching efficiency. In this area it is really no better than Google or Yahoo. **Rating=4**

4. Clusty, www.clusty.com

This search service, formally known as Vivisimo, is a useful and efficient meta-search engine. Clusty has both an excellent filtering system and clustering capability, which break out the subcategories of search within the main search. Additionally, Clusty includes the sources of its search hits and links to other data such as news, images, Wikipedia, blogs, and jobs.

Clusty has recently added a feature called Clusty Cloud. This allows users to instantly visualize a topic using a tag cloud display. The Clusty Cloud can create a topic cloud based on any subject of inquiry. Clusty Clouds are created using Clusty search results for the topic that you enter. Since the cloud tags from Clusty, you can click on any of them to go to Clusty search results. Because the clusters are generated in real time, using Clusty to generate the cloud also ensures that it is always up to date. The Clusty Cloud may be used for any purpose, and is in my opinion significantly better than cloud generators available from other search engines. Clusty is one of the best search engines available on the Internet and produces consistently relevant search results. **Rating=5**

Clusty introduces Clustering 2.0

5. Iseek, www.iseek.com

This meta-search engine has clustering and a good filter that gives consistently helpful results, Iseek has an advanced clustering capability which not only lists topics but also clusters by places, organizations, date and time, abbreviations, the date of publication of the results, and a listing of the sources of results.

With a few improvements, Iseek could become a top of the line search engine. **Rating=4**

6. Ask, www.ask.com

Formally known as Ask Jeeves, this search engine features helpful search tools such as images, news, maps, weather, encyclopedias, and blogs. Ask.com has also recently added a preview of sites explored that includes snapshots and statistics. This preview is shown by a binocular symbol next to the results. I do, however, consider Ask.com to be average in its efficacy, and thus users may be able to do better by going elsewhere. **Rating=3.5**

7. Dogpile, www.dogpile.com

Dogpile is a metasearch engine that searches Google, Yahoo, MSN and Ask, all at the same time. This search engine also features a "favorite fetches" list that details the day's most common searches on Dogpile.

On the top of the Dogpile homepage, there are tabs for the Web, images, audio, video, news, the yellow pages and the white pages.

On the positive side, both Dogpile's search filter and its search results seem quite good. However, the lack of clustering and other essential tools do not help to differentiate Dogpile that significantly from other general, popular search engines. **Rating=3.5**

8. MSN Search, www.msn.com

This visually striking search-enabled homepage is one of the most attractive startup pages of any search engine. The top of the page has the standard tabs for Web, images, news, local shopping, and Q&A beta. In addition, the page has illustrated links to such topics as video highlights, entertainment, popular searches, local weather, money, shopping, MSN news, and sports. However, in my opinion, all of this interesting content masks a very mediocre search engine that delivers poor results. MSN Live Search actually has produced some of the worst results of any of the search engines I have ever used.

All is not entirely lost, however, with MSN search. There is a helpful section called "live Q&A beta." Q&A links the search inquiry you placed in MSN Live Search into an engine that shows answers to your question provided by other members of the MSN community. For example, I entered the question, "why does a dog bark?" and got back 32 answers from other MSN members who had dog barking problems. Q&A beta shows great promise but is not useful enough to offset MSN Live Search engine's poor results. **Rating=1**

9. Qksearch, www.qksearch.com

This metasearch engine has interesting features that can be very useful during searching. Qksearch states that it is the "world's only 3-in-1 metasearch engine." Indeed Qksearch is the only search engine I know of that offers three ways of viewing search results. It features the clustering search (similar to EZ2find or Clusty), the blended search, and the split search.

When I investigated the clustered search I found interesting capabilities. Qksearch can list results both by popularity and relevancy. Additionally, Qksearch can be translated to several languages including English, French, German, Italian and Dutch. In addition, Qksearch incorporates fancy writing tools some similar to those used in word processing. Another interesting feature is the ability to switch between search modes within the search results page.

The per engine search feature (split search) allows for the most popular results to be shown from a variety of search engines, such as Fast, MSN, and Yahoo. This useful feature allows users to see the differences in results between the major search engines.

The blended search feature on the start page of Qksearch shows the results of a "standard" type of search. In my opinion, Qksearch shows great promise as a browser due to its interesting search capabilities and available tools but is ultimately only slightly better at search filtering than any average search engine. Despite this problem Qksearch is still worth a try. **Rating=3.5**

10. Flexfinder Metasearch, www.flexfinder.com

This useful metasearch engine has tabs on the start page for links to the open directory, news, Government, blogs, the Web, health and medicine, and research and education. Flexfinder queries second, third and fourth tier search engines during its search as well as several major directories. It comes up with interesting results that are usually different from those produced by one of the larger search engines.

The layout of results retrieved from Flexfinder is quite clear. A tab next to the result allows for a connection to the Internet archive at http://web.archive.org, which will show stored results.

The Flexfinder search engine has a good filtering mechanism that displays a small number of relevant results. In my opinion, Flexfinder Meta-search shows great promise as a search engine, and could be within the top-tier if it incorporated the tools, such as clustering, that are available with other search engines. **Rating=3.5**

11. Ixquick Metasearch, www.ixquick.com

This metasearch engine was one of the first available on the Internet. Search opetions available from the Ixquick start page include an international phone directory, lowest shopping price search, and picture search. Ixquick metasearch is a comprehensive tool that draws its results from eight search engines, including "all the Web," Ask, "entire Web," Gigablast, MSN, Go, Netscape, and the open directory. When used as a search engine, Ixquick will show the 30 unique top-ten pages from the matching results. Recently, Ixquick also added a feature where all search data is deleted within forty eight hours. This is an excellent step forward in preventing potential data mining which may occur from saved searches.

On the downside, Ixquick has not moved forward by incorporating advanced features (such as clustering), and their search results are not particularly remarkable or well filtered. It is, therefore, not among the search engines I would personally use for a metasearch. **Rating=3.5**

12. Mamma Metasearch, www.mamma.com

This is yet another search engine that has been around for a long time on the Internet. Mamma's home page has tabs that link to the Web, news, images, yellow pages and white pages, "Mamma Career Search," and "Mamma Health."

Mamma's search filtering mechanism shows a small, reliable number of results and suggestions for ways to further refine the search. Mamma, like Ixquick, lacks the advanced features of the other top metasearch engines, but is still a decent, usable choice for a metasearch engine. **Rating=2.5**

13. Gigablast Metasearch, www.gigablast.com

This popular metasearch engine contributes to the search results of most other metasearch engines. There are links on Gigablast's front page to the Web, directory, blogs, travel and Government. Gigablast's metasearch produces its results in an interesting way. Once a result is found, an item called "Gigabits" appears above the result, which classifies the search findings via percentages that rank the relevancy of the various words found in the search results. For example under the search term, "why does a dog bark," Giga bits showed 70% for "barking," 55% for "dogs," 44% for "collars, 29% for "dogs bark," and 25% for "barks." This is a unique feature that analyzes a cross-section of the terms that are present within the results of the search.

A researcher can view Gigablast results in standard, cached, or stripped format. Search findings are shown with links related to the search on both the left and the right of the result. In addition, the search result itself is shown in detail with Gigabit words highlighted in the search. The actual search result generated by

Gigablast seemed about average in comparison to other metasearch engines and were not exceptional. **Rating=4.5**

14. iBoogie Metasearch, www.iboogie.com

This is a new release, still in Beta testing. This metasearch engine has tabs on its starting page that link to the Web, directory, images, and news. It has the added ability to allow users to insert a custom tab, such as medical, Government, library science, or jobs. At last count, iBoogie used 174 search sources, well above the amount accessed by a standard metasearch engine.

When a search is conducted using iBoogie there are clusters of results on the left, and related directory topics on the top of the search results. The search results themselves were listed along with the origins of the sites that originally listed the search (this feature is present with most metasearch engines).

The iBoogie search filter produced a small amount of targeted answers to search inquiries. In my opinion, iBoogie is a useful metasearch engine and ranks among the best of the metasearch engines reviewed. **Rating=3.5**

15. GrabAll Metasearch, www.graball.com

This metasearch engine has links on the start page to: Web, images, news, video, price, reference, software, map, local, people, and weather. These links are more diverse and useful than those on most other metasearch engines. GrabAll metasearch draws results from a large number of search engines such as Google, Yahoo, Ask, MSN, DMOZ, Gigablast, and Looksmart. When GrabAll metasearch is used, any two of the incorporated search engines can be placed side by side and the results compared. This is a unique and useful feature, but in my opinion, GrabAll is still an average metasearch engine that lacks the advanced features present in other top metasearch engines. **Rating=3.5**

16. Nextaris Metasearch, www.nextaris.com

Nextaris is billed as an all-in-one toolkit for searching the Web, tracking news, capturing Web content, and sharing. **Rating=NA**

17. Kartoo Metasearch, www.kartoo.com

This unusual metasearch engine displays its results in the form of a map. When a search is conducted on Kartoo, a map is created around the central concepts of the search results.

On the left side of the map there is a list of the main topics that are covered by the search. In my opinion, Kartoo is confusing to use, and its mapping technology does not add much to its searching capabilities. **Rating=3.5**

18. Cometquery Metasearch, www.cometquery.com

Cometquery has links on its front page for search, audio, images, and the Web. Cometquery shows the results of the search juxtaposed with a snapshot of the Website that it targeted in the search. While this feature is innovative, there is still nothing that remarkable about Cometquery. **Rating=3**

19. Grokker Metasearch, www.grokker.com

This primarily Enterprise search tool can be used by individuals who wish to take advantage of its interesting abilities and valuable results. One of the problems with Grokker is that it uses a maximum of only three search mechanisms: Yahoo, Wikipedia and Amazon. In my opinion, this lack of sources tends to limit the usefulness of Grokker's results. Grokker, however, does have some interesting capabilities. Once a search is conducted using Grokker, there are two viewing possibilities, the outline or the map view. Grokker's outline view shows a clustering of results next to the actual Websites within the cluster. Detail of the results can be set to less, medium (default) or more. As an alternative, Grokker's map view produces maps that show results similar to those in a clustered search engine. Once a circle (cluster) is opened, the researcher finds the results of the search inside. This is a useful feature but the same confusing look found on Kartoo.

One of problems with Grokker is that it only incorporates three search mechanisms, Yahoo, Wikipedia and Amazon. This lack of sources limits the comprehensiveness of Grokker's results. In my opinion, Grokker has a great idea but needs more improvement to become a top search engine. **Rating=3**

20. Incywincy, www.incywincy.com

This top of the line invisible Web search engine yields interesting but inconsistent results. Incywincy has links on its start page to the Web, forms, images, and directories. Search results are listed along with other possibilities that can narrow your search. Incywincy has a decent search filter with fewer results than a regular search engine. It can produce extraordinary results and is an excellent addition to any search. **Rating=4.5**

INCYWINCY
THE INVISIBLE WEB SEARCH ENGINE

Web Forms Directory

| Search |

Advanced Search
Preferences
Safe Search Off
Create Account

Learn more about IncyWincy

Powered by Net Research Server ©2007 LoopIP LLC | Listings & Keywords

21. Carrot Clustering Engine, currently in beta testing, www. carrot2.org

This new search engine has some promise, but it is not up to the search performance levels of either Clusty.com or ez2find. com. On the front page there are links to the Web, news, Wiki's, ODP, jobs, and other useful links. I believe that a final judgment of this search engine cannot be performed until it leaves beta testing. **Rating=NA**

The choice of search engine is one of the most important steps in improving the quality of your search result. In this chapter, I have profiled what I believe are the best Meta, Specialty, and Invisible Web search engines available on the Web today. If a reader chooses one of the top rated search engines listed, their search will be quicker, more efficient, and more thorough than if they had used one of the more popular standard search engines.

CHAPTER 6:
THE PUBLIC LIBRARY: KEY TO FREE RESEARCH

A common problem for researchers is how to find comprehensive, pay-based commercial databases without having to pay a fee for the content.

A few years ago, everything on the Internet was free because it was ad based. Now, unfortunately, most commercial databases charge for access. However, there is a "secret" way to access high quality, pay-based, commercial databases for free: get a local library card. Your local public library card, originally a key only to the world of books, can now also deliver the world of commercial, pay-based, expensive search content to you at no cost.

Because many libraries do not advertise their premium online services, library members often have no inkling of the enormous value of the content available in their local library system. Libraries license low cost, high quality commercial databases to themselves, allowing all members of that library system to access these databases from anywhere with an internet connection. Library databases can run the gamut of subjects from business and news services to vehicles, and are almost always invisible Web databases. Depending upon the diversity of databases offered, and the amount of money allocated by the library to fund access to them, the value of the databases may be well in excess of $50,000. Of course, libraries differ significantly and some (typically, those in affluent areas, or servicing large cities) may have a huge amount of offerings, while others have very few.

Depending upon where you live, it may be possible to get several different library cards. Your library card number can then be used as a key to unlock the databases licensed to the local library for patron use. I encourage the readers to get as many library cards as they are legally entitled to apply for, since the available databases may vary from library to library. There is truly something for everyone online at your local Public Library.

I will now list and describe, in alphabetical order, many of the databases that are typically available at a local public library. Given the almost countless number of libraries in the United States, this list is by no means a complete list of all online library databases, but is intended to be representative of what can usually be found.

For my first group of available resources, I have chosen the offerings of the Brooklyn Public Library, located online at www. brooklynpubliclibrary.org. This library serves over six million people in the borough of Brooklyn and beyond, and is known colloquially as the "Everyman's Library."

AVAILABLE FROM THE BROOKLYN, NY, PUBLIC LIBRARY

1. ABI Inform Research

ABI Inform Research is a scholarly business periodicals database that uses over 1,750 North American sources to provide information on business topics such as advertising, economics, finance, marketing, computers, etc. This database is a part of the Proquest group of databases. ABI Inform research may be searched separately or along with Proquest newspapers. ABI Inform also has access to information on over 60,000 companies, with information dating back to 1971. Samples of the publications covered by ABI Inform Research include: Management World (Washington, D.C.), Managing Office Technology (Cleveland), Money Magazine (New York), Scientific American (New York), Supermarket Business (New York), and of course, the Wall Street Journal (New York). Many of the databases covered by ABI Inform Research are full text in nature. ABI Inform Research is an excellent source of data for anyone seeking information on business from magazines, newspapers and other periodicals.
Rating=4

2. Academic Search Premiere

This EBSCO Host research database is the world's largest academic, multidisciplinary database. It is updated on a daily basis and provides full text for nearly 4,650 serials, including more than 3,600 peer reviewed titles. Files date back as far as 1975 and are digitally stored in PDF form. Articles are available from over 100 journals, and feature searchable, cited references for more than 1,000 titles. Academic Search Premiere offers academic journals covering all major areas of study, including, Social Sciences, Humanities, Education, Computer Science, Arts & Literature, and many more.

EBSCO host has a very interesting feature known as Visual Search, which returns a visual map of your search. The visual map contains circles that represent sub categories of your original search, and squares which represent articles within the circles. This is powered by the search engine Grokker (discussed in the previous chapter). **Rating=3.5**

3. America the Beautiful

This is a state by state history and current events site aimed at elementary and middle school students. This database is a Grolier Online Passport member, and includes Encyclopedia American, La Nueva Encyclopedia Cumbre, The New Book of Popular Science, Land and Peoples, and America the Beautiful, all in a single interface. In addition, there is search capability for the entire "Passport group," "this day in history," "News Now," international news, world newspapers, and "From the Editor's Desk." **Rating=3**

4. Associations Unlimited

This database is a directory of international, national, regional, state, and local non-profit organizations. This resource is part of the Infotrac Group published by Thomson Gale. Users may search Associations Unlimited by name or acronym, location, subject, SIC Code, postal code or telephone area code, or Boolean search terms. In addition to all of this valuable information, a researcher can search Internal Revenue Service data on U.S. non-profit, 501-C status organizations. **Rating=3**

5. The Biography and Genealogy Master Index

This Infotrac database is a first stop tool for finding biographical material on people from all time periods, geographic locations, and fields of endeavor. The Biography and Genealogy Master Index catalogs any product that includes biographical information on people. Using the Biography and Genealogy Master Index is relatively simple. All you have to do is to enter the first few letters of the desired subject's last name in the search box, and press the search button for results. **Rating=3.5**

6. Biography Reference Bank

This H.W. Wilson database has information on people from antiquity to the present and a comprehensive image bank. This database can be used along with the Library Literature and Full Text database, which will be described later in this chapter. When I used this database, I requested a search under the term "Roosevelt." I got the top-ten results, an 80 confidence rating, descriptions of Eleanor, Franklin, and Theodore Roosevelt, and a variety of pictures. **Rating=3.5**

7. Book Index with Reviews

This Galenet database allows users to find titles that are in print, out of print, or soon to be published. It is searchable by item of literature, contemporary authors, or contemporary literary criticism. **Rating=3.5**

8. BooksinPrint.com Professional

This interesting database has over five million book, audio book, and video titles available for search, along with a growing number of recent Federal Government publications. A researcher can search the database by keyword, book type, title, author, and publisher, or browse it by general subject area. There is also a new section called "Fiction Connection," where the database recommends titles similar to those you are reading. Additionally, there is a connection to author video interviews at Book Rap Central and Book Wire, the comprehensive online portals to the book industry. This database is also available in a Spanish edition that searches for Spanish language titles. **Rating=3.5**

9. The Business and Company Resource Center

This Galenet database is an excellent source of company profiles, brand information, rankings, investment reports, histories, chronologies, and periodicals. The database is searchable by company, industry, articles, or advanced search. Once a company is entered into the database, a wide variety of information is available pertaining to the company, including company profiles, news and magazine articles, histories, investment reports, financial reports, rankings, suits and claims, products, industry overview, etc. Overall this database is an excellent source of information on businesses. **Rating=4.5**

10. Business Source Premiere

This EBSCO host database searches for citations from and full text versions of articles from many different sources. These sources include: academic journals, trade publications, magazines, books, company profiles, SWOT analysis, country reports, industry profiles, market research reports, and product reviews. The basic search mechanism is Boolean in nature, and thus search results tend to be too broad in scope to make this an entirely efficient search mechanism for this type of data. However, in spite of these difficulties, this database does produce interesting results. **Rating=4**

11. Corporate Resource Net

This EBSCO host database is similar in scope and design to Business Source Premiere; the type of material covered is quite different. Corporate Resource Net covers articles from general business magazines and top management journals. In addition, Corporate Resource Net also includes detailed company profiles for 5,000 of the world's largest corporations. Included publications include: periodicals, newspapers, books, and journals. Articles can be searched with either PDF or text with graphic images included. This database, similar to Business Source Premiere, is also powered by a Boolean search engine, which leads to a large amount of hits per inquiry. As with Business Source Premiere, the results gathered from this database are of a high enough quality to recommend its use. **Rating=4**

12. Credo Reference

This new database has been showing up in libraries around the nation. It features full text articles for over 200 reference sources spanning diverse subjects. This database includes maps, images, and other interesting add-ons. This site was formerly known as XRFER Plus, a commercial database. **Rating=4**

13. Custom Newspapers

This Gale database is a collection of over 150 national and international newspapers searchable by subject, key word, or the entire document. At last count, Custom Newspapers has over 27,900,000 papers, impressive by any database standard.

When using Custom Newspapers, the search results tend to be extremely interesting, due to the proliferation of foreign newspapers which are generally unknown to the average American citizen. My sample search for IBM came up with items from London, England's Daily Mirror, Daily Telegraph, The Financial Times and The Guardian. In addition, The New Delhi Economic Times (India) also appeared as a result. Due to the availability of Custom Newspapers' unusual content, this database is a recommended source for periodical information from both the U.S. and abroad. **Rating=4.5**

14. Encyclopedia Americana

This is an in-depth reference source is a member of the Grolier Online Passport Family. This database includes articles, Web links, and information on current events. **Rating=2**

15. Encyclopedia Britannica/Academic Edition

Encyclopedia Britannica is perhaps one of the best known and most comprehensive of all encyclopedias. This is a full version of encyclopedia Britannica that is updated on a continual basis. After entering the site, there are three columns of information and a search box on top. The search takes place either in Encyclopedia Britannica online, or in Merriam Webster Dictionary and Thesaurus. On the left column, there is a list of research tools, including an index, an A to Z browse, a subject browse, a world atlas, timelines, the "Year in Review," world data, video browse, notable quotations and the "Gateway to Classics." In the center of the page, one finds "Britannica Highlights," a "Biography of the Day," and "This Day in History." On the right hand side of the page, there are links to current items from the New York Times online, BBC News and SBS World News. Based on the quality searches as well as the vast amount of information available, this is a highly recommended site, especially for students. **Rating=4**

16. Encyclopedia Britannica/Annals of American History

This database is full of interesting documents on American history from 1493 to today. In this resource, you can click a timeline for a specific period to see selections from those years. You may also browse by author or by topics of American history, or search the entire database. **Rating=4**

17. The Encyclopedia Britannica/Online World Data Analyst

This database offers statistical portraits of the nations of the world, as well as tools for making comparative charts and tables. **Rating=4**

18. ERIC

This EBSCO database has full text articles, citations and abstracts from the current Index of Journals in Education, Resources in Education Index, and other education related catalogs.

This database can be adjusted for its intended audience, catering to either administrators, community counselors, or teachers. **Rating=3**

19. Ferguson's Career Guidance Center

This unusual database is a comprehensive career research database organized by industry, providing profiles of today's most popular jobs. This database covers careers and career resources, as well as career preparation information such as scholarships, academic / non-academic programs, Web resources and an employability skills checklist. The information provided by this database is both useful and in depth. It is an excellent stop for anyone looking for a job. **Rating=4**

20. The Gale Virtual Reference Library

This database features encyclopedias, almanacs, and specialized sources for multi-disciplinary research. The reference materials comprising this database used to be available only in the library, but can now be accessed remotely. This database creates is own e-book collection, based on the library that hosts it. Upon examination and use of this database, it is my opinion that due to its narrow focus and insufficient number of sources, one should utilize this database in addition to broader and more comprehensive database sources. **Rating=4**

21. Health Reference Center Academic

This Gale database has over 2,800,000 articles, covering academic journals, magazines, reference, news, and multimedia. The database is a comprehensive search mechanism for all types of health related information. Even everyday medical problems, such as athlete's foot, are covered. **Rating=3**

22. Health Source Consumer Edition

This EBSCO database has full text articles, indices, and abstracts about health. You may search by either pamphlet, periodical, book, or all sources. I have found that this database produces excellent results on a number of topics, with both HTML full text and PDF results. **Rating=3**

23. History Reference Center

This EBSCO database features historical maps, pictures and full text articles, and is updated monthly. The database is searchable by timelines of world and U.S. history, such as "world history," "early civilizations," and "the years 4,000 B.C. to 1,000 B.C." It is also adjustable to the Lexile reading level of users, and to grades five to eight, and nine to twelve. In addition, images are available in either PDF or text with graphics. The History Reference Center offers the digitized full text versions of over 1,000 text books, encyclopedias, and non-fiction books; cover to cover full text for sixty history magazines, 58,000 historical documents, 43,000 biographies of historical figures, more than 12,000 historical photos and maps, and more than 80 hours of historical videos. I highly recommend this database to all interested parties, especially teachers of world and American history, and junior, middle and senior high school students. **Rating=3.5**

24. Informe

This Gale database is a full text Spanish database. It covers culture, technology, health, and other materials. It has over 3,400,000 articles in Spanish and searches academic journals, magazines, reference books, news, and multimedia. **Rating=3.5**

25. Lands and Peoples Online

This Grolier Passport database allows you to search either all of Grolier Online, or Lands and Peoples only. It is an encyclopedia of countries, cultures, and current events that is appropriate for middle and high school students. It allows for search by news desk, atlas, cross culture, passport, and area of the world. It also features a teacher's guide to enhance its answers. **Rating=3.5**

26. The Learning Express Library

This extremely interesting database requires free registration in addition to your library membership. This database has test prep material and practice exams for a number of standardized tests. Among the tests covered are high school Advanced Placement exams, Civil Service exams, and college entrance exams such as the ACT and the new SAT. In addition, there are practice exams and test prep material on Cosmetology, e-books, elementary level skills, middle school skills, Military testing (ASVAB), Nursing, reading comprehension, real estate, resume preparation and interviewing, GED, Graduate Schools entrance exams (GRE, MCAT, LSAT, GMAT), math skills, Spanish language, teaching CBEST and PPST, TOEFL, U.S. Citizenship and health careers. This unique database is highly recommended as a source on information for those individuals who may be taking exams in any of the aforementioned areas, their parents, or their teachers. **Rating=4.5**

27. The Library Literature and Information Science Full Text

This H.W. Wilson bibliographic database may be used separately or in conjunction with the previously described Biography Reference Bank. This database indexes articles and book reviews in more than 23 key library and information science periodicals published across the world. When used, answers to this database were ranked by confidence, and had primarily full text PDF capability. **Rating=3**

28. The Literary Reference Center

This database provides information on thousands of authors and works collected from reference works, books, and literary journals. It includes the following: plot summaries, literary criticisms, book reviews, author biographies and interviews, full text articles from literary journals, and images. **Rating=3.5**

29. MasterFile Premiere

This EBSCO, multidisciplinary database, which was designed specifically for public libraries, provides full text for more than 1,700 general reference publications dating back to 1975. MasterFile Premiere also includes about 500 full text reference books, 84,000 biographies, 100,000 primary source documents and an image collection of over 200,000 photos, maps, and flags. Once a search is entered into MasterFile Premiere, it is possible to either see all results together, or results divided by their publication of origin (periodicals, newspapers, reference books, pamphlets, biographies, primary source documents, and images). I have personally found that results of searches using this database are quite good, and include HTML full text and PDF files. My only problem with this database is the potential for too many hits on a particular search. **Rating=4**

30. The McClatchy Tribune Collection

The EBSCO host database has a 90 day archive of approximately 100 newspapers from the McClatchy Tribune collection. The available newspapers include: The Daily Camera of Boulder, Colorado; The News and Observer of Raleigh, N. C.; The San Jose Mercury News; The Charlotte Observer; Newsday, New York; and numerous others. Most results are in HTML full text. **Rating=4**

31. Middle Search Plus

Middle Search Plus also provides full text of over 140 popular magazines for middle and junior high school audiences. All full text articles included in the database are assigned a reading level indicator (Exiles) and offers full text information dating to 1990. Middle Search Plus also contains over 84,000 biographies, over 100,000 primary source documents, and an image collection of over 200,000 photos, maps, and flags. This database is updated daily on BSCO host, and is an excellent source of data for middle school and junior high school students. **Rating=4**

32. The National Newspaper Index

This Infotrac database has full text articles and an index of the New York Times, the Wall Street Journal, the Christian Science Monitor, the L.A. Times and the Washington Post. The National Newspaper index has almost 5 million articles in its database, and is an excellent source of data for financially based queries. **Rating=4.5**

33. Natural Medicines Comprehensive Database, Consumer Version

Natural Medicines describes herbal remedies, dietary supplements, vitamins, and the like. When searching Natural Medicines, you may enter any natural product name, disease, condition, or drug name, and get objective product information, effectiveness ratings, and potential interaction with other drugs. Considering the rapid growth of holistic and alternative medicine in today's society, this is a very useful database. **Rating=4**

34. The New Book of Knowledge

The New Book of Knowledge is a member of the Grolier On-line Passport of databases. This resource includes reference, current events, maps, photos, flags, Web links, and homework help. This database is intended for student readers from elementary school up through high school. **Rating=2.5**

35. The New Book of Popular Science

This is yet another member of the Grolier family. It is an in-depth science resource, including projects and experiments. The information contained within is appropriate for grade K through twelfth. It is a boon to parents looking to help their kids with those last minute science fair projects! **Rating=3**

36. New York State Newspapers

This Galenet database has over 1,000,000 articles culled from ten major papers in New York state, including: Newsday, The New York Post, The Times Herald Record (Middletown), The Times Union of Albany, and others. Libraries in other states may offer similar collections of local newspapers. **Rating=4**

37. The New York Times

This Proquest database features full text articles and abstracts of The New York Times from 1980 to the present. This is an excellent catalog of "the newspaper of record." **Rating=4.5**

38. News Paper Source

This EBSCO host database is updated daily, and provides selected full text for nearly 30 national and international newspapers. This database also contains full text television and radio news transcripts and selected full text for more than 20 United States newspapers. This database is searchable by newspaper, news wire, transcript, or all, and includes articles with images. This database has produced excellent results for numerous searches the I performed. **Rating=4.5**

39. NoveList

This electronic resource enables users to find new authors and titles. On top of the home page, there is "This month's tips and tidbits" along with links to recommended books and discussion guides. One can also search the database, browse lists, check out the Reader for Readers column, and review a Reader's Advisory regarding newer publications. This database is relatively unknown and obscure but would likely prove quite interesting to the avid fiction reader. **Rating=3**

40. Nueva Enciclopedia Cumbre en Linea

This Grolier Online Passport entry is a complete encyclopedia for Spanish speakers and Spanish language students. It includes grammar, vocabulary and news from the Spanish press. The material covered by this encyclopedia is appropriate for all age groups. **Rating=4**

41. Primary Search

This EBSCO database provides full text for nearly 70 popular magazines for elementary school research. All full text articles included in this database are assigned a Lexile reading level indicator, and full text information dates as far back as 1990. **Rating=4**

42. Professional Development Collection

This EBSCO database features articles and abstracts from academic journals for professional educators. This is one of a few databases available that targets the professional educator.
Rating=3.5

43. Reference USA

This useful database is one of the best for demographic research that I have ever seen. Recently updated with a new look, Reference USA now has even more information, including deep, invisible Web information. The available databases for reference USA are: Business, with over 14,000,000 U.S. businesses; Residential, with over 120,000,000 households; and Healthcare, with 835,000 Physicians and Dentists. There is also a Canadian section with 1,300,000 Canadian businesses and 12,000,000 Canadian residential households.

The typical personal search occurs by name, state and city. The information typically shown after a search is the name, address, city, state, and zip code, county, phone number, median household income, median home value, longitude and latitude, percentage of owner occupied housing, map or driving directions. Another interesting included feature is the ability to show you your neighbors within a tenth of a mile to a five mile radius of your home.

The business section of Reference USA is also a unique and valuable resource. It is difficult to get any reliable information on privately held companies. Reference USA, through their business search, provides information on privately held businesses that would be otherwise difficult or expensive to acquire. A typical business search for a small, privately held business will yield the general information provided by phonebooks (address, name, phone number), and then a deeper level of information that includes the type of business, the primary SIC code, and the NAICS code.

In addition, corporate information is provided, such as the number of employees, estimated annual sales, type of business, location, credit rating, Website, home business or public company, year established, yellow page ad spending, hours of operation and acceptance of credit cards. Reference USA also has a corporate family tree (not applicable for most small business), a company description, a management directory, a summary of recent company news, and, most importantly, a UCC profile that shows property pledged as collateral to creditors and any public filings.

In addition to all of this extremely valuable information, there is one capability that Reference USA has that makes it stand out even more: searchers, using the radius function in the map and direction section, may find any type of business, either by SIC or NAICS number from one-tenth of a mile to five miles away from the location. I teach a small business course at the college level and all of my students are required to include in their sample business plans, a survey of competitors using information from Reference USA. This site also has a health care section, where you may find most practicing Dentists or Doctors. This information includes the age of the doctors, office manager, schools graduated from, and number of prescriptions written. **Rating=5**

44. Regional Business News

This EBSCO host database provides comprehensive, full text coverage for regional business publications. Regional business news has over 75 business journals, newspapers, and news wires, from all metropolitan and rural areas within the United States. **Rating=4.5**

45. The Science Resource Center

The Science Resource Center covers curriculum related science topics, and offers teachers an easy to use tool, to identify content directly related to state and national standards. This is vital for all teacher of science, regardless of the level that they teach. **Rating=3.5**

46. Serials Directory

This EBSCO host database provides access to the most up-to-date and accurate bibliographic information, as well as current pricing structures for popular serials. It contains over 212,000 titles, including newspapers and data from over 100,000 publishers worldwide, as well as E-mail and Internet addresses. **Rating=3**

47. Student Resource Center

This Galenet database features primary documents, biographies, essays, and analysis on a variety of topics. Student Resource Center also includes photos, illustrations, and audio and video clips. Students can conduct searches in topic areas such as geography and culture, history, literature, person search, and science and health. **Rating=4**

48. Twaynes Author's Series

This Galenet database has biographical information on over 200 U.S. and English authors, including full text discussions on the authors' works, and a chronology of the authors lives. **Rating=3.5**

As a researcher, I have found that one of the most difficult problems with library research is choosing the correct database to find answers to my search query. The Brooklyn Public Library, as well as several other libraries, has attempted to solve this problem by permitting a search using all available databases. Once that search is created, any particular hits on any database in the library's catalog will be shown. The big problem with this solution is that you may have too much material to sort through, including much material that is likely to be superfluous to your needs. Despite this problem, the All Search Function is very useful for a researcher.

As stated at the beginning of this chapter, there are many libraries available, with many different database offerings. In order to get a true picture of what offerings are available from library to library, I will now describe the offerings of the public library system from Queens, New York. I will only describe those offerings that differ from the Brooklyn, NY, Public Library system.

The Queens, NY, Public Library system, located at www. queenslibrary.org, is the third largest library system in New York City, serving approximately three million patrons. According to the National Geographic Society, Queens contains the most culturally and ethnically diverse population in the world, its library system must be both superlative in content and highly user friendly. The Queens library has recently taken great strides in increasing its database offerings. I truly believe that it is one of the premiere online library research collections available in the nation.

THE QUEENS, NY, PUBLIC LIBRARY SYSTEM

1. The African American Experience

This database is an online collection of authoritative reference works, primary sources, images, and audio clips about African American life. You may browse by various subjects such as business, history music, religion, sports, and other countries. In addition, primary documents, including letters, narration and text, are available. **Rating=3.5**

2. The Children's Literature Comprehensive Database

This database may be searched either by full text, search word, major qualifiers (such as category), genre, or by special qualifiers (such as author or illustrator). **Rating=3**

3. College Source Online

This database is a virtual library that represents over 34,000 college catalogues in full cover to cover original page format, with two-year, four-year, graduate, professional and international schools highlighted. This database can be extremely useful when you are comparing colleges prior to applying. **Rating=4.5**

4. Bowker's BooksinPrint.com and Global BooksinPrint.com

Bowker's Books in Print.com includes links to the fiction connection, where you may discover titles similar to the books that you already read. Other sections include the Fiction Room, the Children's Room, Your Favorites and, What Year Were You Born? Here, you may enter any date in the past century to read about what happened that year, and see what books were best sellers. This database may also be quick-searched or browsed by subject or author. Global Books in Print.com has a database of over 11 million books, audio books, and video titles. Global Books in Print includes publishers' catalogues online at each publisher's home page, Book Wire, and a comprehensive online portal with detailed information about the book industry. You may also view author video interviews at Book Wrap Central. This database may be quick-searched, by market, general subject, or index. **Rating=3.5**

5. Lawchek Online

Lawchek Online is a reference product designed for both the layperson and the attorney. Eleven areas of law are currently included in this database: bankruptcy, contracts, corporations, criminal law, domestic/family law, education, intellectual property, landlord-tenant, real estate, trial litigation, and wills and estates.

In each discipline area, you may access state specific information from either the help guide or the form section. This database is extremely user friendly and offers simple answers to every day questions. A glossary of common legal terms is also provided. In addition, personal legal source books, which describe different disciplines of law, are available, as well as letter pro, which helps you to find letter templates for use at home and at work. Lawchek Online is a very useful database that is only available for libraries. **Rating=4**

6. Litfinder

This Galenet database enables users to browse for poems, stories, essays, plays, speeches, and authors, or by genre, subject, and contemporary work. There is an "author of the month" area, a kid's corner, and a search mechanism. **Rating=3.5**

7. Opposing Viewpoints Resource Center

This database is a one-stop source for information on today's hottest social issues. The Opposing Viewpoints Resource Center features viewpoint articles, topic overviews, full text magazine and newspaper articles, primary source documents, images and pod casts, statistics, and links to Websites. Opposing Viewpoint is an Infotrac database. **Rating=4**

8. Standard and Poor's Net Advantage

Net Advantage's opening page includes a synopsis of today's market, market news, bonds, the economy, investment ideas, industries, and funds. This database may be searched by either publication ticker or keyword. In addition, there are quick links to industry surveys, Standard and Poor's Outlook, and Net Advantages Guides. When a company is searched a business summary comes up along with links to the company's profile, vital statistics, stock reports, corporation records, bond reports, industry surveys, and sub-industry news. I have personally found when you use Net Advantage you achieve comprehensive results. **Rating=4.5**

9. Student Resource Center Silver

This Informal database contains thousand of curriculum oriented primary documents, biographies, topical essays, background information, critical analysis, and full text coverage of over 650 magazines and newspapers. It also features more than 20,000 photographs and illustrations and over eight hours of audio and video clips. **Rating=4**

10. SIRS Knowledge Source Comprehensive Search Portal

This Proquest database is perhaps one of the most useful and comprehensive databases offered through any library system. The power, quality of results and ease of use of this database can never be underestimated. It is one of my personal favorites whenever I have to conduct research. Basically, SIRS knowledge source is a combination of three separate SIRS databases. The first being SIRS researcher, which covers student reference, social issues, health, science and business. The second database is SIRS Government Reporter, which has both historic, and Government documents, directories, and almanacs. The third is SIRS Discoverer, which is a general reference database that is designed for young researchers.

SIRS Knowledge source may be searched by either subject heading or key word natural language, and may be sorted by either relevance, or date. In addition, there are tabs on the top of the page for advanced search, a topic browse, and the features of each database. Above that, there are links to "My Research," which will show you the history of what you have researched, educator's resources, and a useful toolbox. Below that there are links to help, how to site, and a dictionary and thesaurus. On the right side of the page, there are links to Top Searches, and features such as Today's News, and other Hot Topics. When used, SIRS Researcher shows a header that shows all of the articles relevant to your search, and then breaks it down into categories of newspapers, magazines, Government documents, primary sources, reference, and graphics. Additionally, it offers the option to show, to hide details, and to sort by relevance, date and lexile. Individual results show the name of the article, a graphic if available, the publication it came from, and the date, the lexile score, and the length of the total article and the SIRS database from which it came. The link to the article may be evoked and the entire article can be both viewed and printed out. If the printing is not desired, then a detailed summary of the article is given. Below this, descriptors are given in the main categories that the article relates to. These descriptors may be clicked on so that additional information may be gathered within the subcategories of the article. My students and I have found that this database produces incredible results on even the most sophisticated of searches, and is a must have, top ten choice among available library databases. **Rating=5**

11. Accunet/AP Photo Archive

This extremely interesting database offers photos from the Civil War to the present, which are searchable by subject, date, or photographer. Once the database is evoked, there are categories from which you may select photos, such as: Today, U.S. News, International News, Sports, Entertainment and Weather. Any photos that are acquired from Accent/AP Photo Archive are license free, and may be used and down loaded as you see fit. In addition, there is a section available for AP Photo and headline, which has photos in many different categories, such as: Showcase, U.S. Weather, World Sports, Entertainment and Business. I have found Accunet/AP PhotoArchive to be an extremely useful source of photos. **Rating=4.5**

12. The Business and Company ASAP

This Infotrac database provides researchers with information on companies markets and industries. This database covers market trends, mergers and acquisitions, and current management theory and company overviews. The site uses business and trade journals, newspapers, and company directory profiles, with full text and images. This database may be invoked only by searching under cross searchable databases when using any other Gale Group database. **Rating=4**

13. Funk and Wagnall's New World Encyclopedia

This EBSCO database is the electronic version of Funk and Wagnall's New World Encyclopedia. In my opinion, which is founded upon examination of the site and the use of the search interface, this database appears to be significantly less useful than the Encyclopedia Britannica. There is also less available data than Encyclopedia Britannica offers. **Rating=2**

14. Infotrac Student Edition/K-12

This Galenet database is a good report source for students from grades K to 12. Using this database is relatively simplistic. All a user must do is enter a subject into the search box, and select the sources that they wish to include in their search, such as: encyclopedias, magazines, maps, newspapers, reference, or all sources. This is a recommended database for those who are in the requested grade levels. **Rating=4**

15. Searchasaurus

This EBSCO host database is, in reality, a relatively sophisticated interface that links a general encyclopedia, middle search plus, Encyclopedia of Animals, a Dictionary, primary search, and pictures into a fun, easy to use database with small islands as search points. The contents in this database are appropriate for grades K to 12. In addition, there is also content aimed at younger students. **Rating=4**

16. SIRS Discover on the Web

This Proquest database is one of several offered under the SIRS name. It allows searching by either subject heading or natural language keyword. This database provides information for class projects, reports or speeches, from magazines, newspapers, and The World Almanac for kids. There are many different subjects that can be browsed, including animals, cultures, history, Government, notable people, science, technology and others. Like other SIRS databases, the results tend to be excellent.
Rating=5

17. World Book Online Encyclopedia

This database is a full version of the well known World Book Encyclopedia. It includes an atlas, a dictionary and educator's tools such as: lessons plans linked to World Book, and travel information such as Explore New York. There are also sections on: feature of the month, behind the headlines, media showcase, today in history, and surf the pages. Even with all of these features, it is not as comprehensive as Encyclopedia Britannica.
Rating=2.5

18. Integrum Worldwide

This database provides access to over 5,000 data sources which focus on the Eurasian nations of Russia [the Commonwealth of Independent States,] and the Baltic States. Full texts of national and regional newspapers and magazines and news archives are also available. Other sources of information include: Official Government documents, Statistical information, Business, industry, market, Government information and directories, as well as Biographies. In addition, there are full texts of thousands of Russian books. **Rating=3.5**

19. Ebsco Animals

Ebsco Animals is an Encyclopedia of Animals, and offers in-depth information on a variety of topics relating to animals. The database consists of indexing, abstracts and full text records which describe the nature and habitat of familiar animals. Within some of the text, image links are available. Images are accessed by double-clicking any image graphic. **Rating=4**

20. Biography & Genealogy Master Index

This database is a great index tool for learning where to look for biographical material on people from all time periods, geographical locations and vocation. **Rating=4.5**

I will now describe the offerings of New York's largest library found in Manhattan on 42nd Street and Fifth Avenue and called The New York Public Library. I will only describe those offerings that differ from the prior two libraries. The address of this library is www.nypl.org.

THE NEW YORK PUBLIC LIBRARY (42ND STREET AND 5TH AVENUE)

1. The Columbia Gazetteer of the World: Online

This database has names descriptions and characteristics of over 165,000 places in the world. Users may search and segment all the information included herein. Search is available by type of place search, place name search, or word search. **Rating=4.5**

2. Ancient and Medieval History Online

This database provides a balanced global view of the ancient world as it explores six ancient centers of civilization: Africa, Egypt, Greece, Rome, Mesoamerica, and Mesopotamia, spanning the period from the earliest Hominids (3-5 million years ago) to 1522. This is a very interesting resource for History teachers and their students, as well as history buffs. **Rating=3**

3. Dictionary of Literary Biography

This database features information on literary figures from all time periods in such genres as fiction, non fiction, poetry, drama, history, and journalism. If you have interest in literature and journalism, then this is the site for you. **Rating=3**

4. History Resources Center, U.S.

This site has a variety of historical data from primary sources, as well as reference documents. It also includes photographs, illustrations, and maps. **Rating=4**

5. History Resource Center, World

This database is a comprehensive collection of reference, full text articles from scholarly publications, and an array of primary source documents. It also includes images, maps and charts, which provide expansive geographic and chronological research materials for the study of world history. World history curricula is supported with over 1,800 primary sources, 27 reference titles, and more than 110 journals. This is a great source of information for teachers, parents, and students. **Rating=4**

6. Library Literature

This site indexes periodicals, books, reports, pamphlets, and library school thesis on all subjects of library and information sciences. **Rating=3**

7. Modern World History Online

This database covers the important civilizations of world history from prehistoric times to the modern era. Topical entries, biographies, maps, primary source documents and time lines, provide a detailed and comparative view of the people, places and events that have defined world history. **Rating=3**

8. Psychology and Behavioral Sciences

This is a full text database of journal articles that cover topics such as psychology, psychiatry, mental processes, anthropology, and experimental methods. **Rating=3.5**

9. Rosetta Stone Learning Center

This unique and well named database requires registration in addition to a valid New York Public Library card. Once accessed, you may examine and learn about other languages in detail. **Rating=4**

10. Science Online

This site covers the fields of animal anatomy, biology, chemistry, computer science, earth science, and many other science areas. Its six categories, diagrams, definitions, biographies, essays, experiments and time lines, are cross referenced through hyper links and are also cross searchable by key word, topic, and year. **Rating=3.5**

As you can see from these comprehensive offerings of three New York City libraries, there is a tremendous amount of valuable content available for free! There is a good chance that your local libraries will offer many of these same resources.

It is hard to know which of your local libraries offers the databases that will be most suitable to your search at any given time; therefore, it is prudent to get as many library cards in your community that you are eligible for.

I will review several other libraries here so you can see additional valuable resources that are typically available in local public libraries.

In Roslyn, New York, there is an excellent library system found at www.nassaulibrary.org. Once there, go to "find your library" and then click on the "R" key and scroll to the library you are seeking. The Roslyn library has the following databases, which are vital to all researchers:

THE ROSLYN, NY, LIBRARY

1. Investext Plus

A Galenet database which is a premiere financial research tool. With a rich backfile to 1982, there are investment company and industry reports from brokers in North American, Europe, Latin America, Asia Pacific, Africa, and the Middle East. All the company and industry reports are provided in the full page, PDF image. **Rating=4.5**

2. Thompson Gale Legal Forms

This database provides a wide selection of state specific and multi state legal forms across the most popular legal areas. This includes: real estate contracts, wills, pre-marital agreements, bankruptcy, landlord Tenants, Divorce, and many others. **Rating=4**

3. Proquest Historical Newspapers/The New York Times 1851-2003

This database may be singly the best newspaper database for historical news that is available today. I realize that most people who are reading this book are not New Yorkers; however, the New York Times is considered one of the nation's greatest, most respected and most well known newspapers. It is difficult to get information as far back as 1851 from any source, let along one as reliable as the New York Times. This database is searchable by basic search [keyword], On This Date, Before This Date, and from [between two dates].

The most amazing capability of this database is that search results yield the actual article, as it was written in the New York Times of that day. Proquest has digitized the entire New York Times from 1851 to 2003 to provide this functionality. I personally use this database for difficult to find original source information on subjects such as the Stock Market Crash of 1929, the Titanic Sinking of 1912, and the Assassination of Abraham Lincoln in 1865. This information is not readily available in the form of primary source documents from any other freely available source. The primary source nature of this site makes this database a must have, must visit resource. **Rating=5+**

4. CultureGrams

This one goes beyond boring facts and figures to deliver an insider's perspective on daily life, culture, history, customs, and lifestyles of the world's people. The growing diversity of America's population, coupled with the new emphasis on global interdependency and multiculturalism, make CultureGrams an indispensable resource for all who seek to better understand the diversity in their nation and their world. **Rating=3.5**

In addition to the database assets of the New York-based libraries that we have discussed, I would also like to go over the assets of other libraries in the Untied States. It should be noted that many libraries have specialties that are indigenous to their region. In addition, many resources that have been mentioned in our prior discussion of libraries are available in libraries throughout the nation, and are considered as somewhat standard resources.

I have chosen several libraries in major metropolitan centers across the United States for discussion and comparison. The first of these is The Boston, Massachusetts, Public Library located at www.bpl.org. This Library seems to emphasize early American History. This is an obvious area of specialty, given the role that the region played in the founding of our nation.

The databases listed here are those that are unique to this library system.

THE BOSTON, MA, PUBLIC LIBRARY

1. Art Museum Image Gallery

This database has over 96,000 high quality art images, with full descriptions gathered from the collections of distinguished museums around the world. Many of the images include curatorial text, provenance data, and related Multi Media. This database covers the entire spectrum of both fine and decorative art. **Rating=4**

2. The Boston Globe, Historical 1872 to 1923

This historical Boston Globe collection offers both full page and article digital images in PDF format, with searchable full text, back to its first issue. This database is similar in scope, but not as comprehensive as the New York Times Historical Edition. **Rating=4.5**

3. Boston Globe, 1980 to Current

This database provides full text articles for staff written news items, feature stories, columns, and editorials from the Boston Globe. This is a good site, yet there is an inexplicable gap between the previous Boston Globe site, which ends in 1923 and this site, which begins in 1980. **Rating=4.5**

4. Business and Management Practices

This is a full text resource with a focus on the practical aspects and approaches of business management. It is updated weekly, and provides coverage back to 1995. It offers information from more than 300 core management journals and trade publications. **Rating=4**

5. D and B Million Dollar Database

This database provides marketing information on more than 14 million U.S. companies. It is searchable by such fields as: SIC and NAICS codes, company size and sales, business type and age, and contact criteria. This database also includes specialty information, such as: Executive name lists and Presidential biographies. One of the best databases of its kind, it is truly comprehensive in scope. **Rating=4.5**

6. Early American Newspapers, Series 1 & 2/1690-1819

This database features cover to cover reproductions of hundreds of historic newspapers, providing more than 1 million pages of fully text searchable facsimile images. This collection has now expanded to include coverage from the western states. **Rating=3**

7. Rare Books

This database is a comprehensive bibliography of rare books that comprises over 600,000 pages of key, out of print bibliographies than can be both browsed and searched online. **Rating=3**

8. Table Base

This database finds market share, company brand rankings, industry and product forecast, production and consumption statistics, imports and exports, usage and capacity, number of users and outlets, trends, and much more. **Rating=4.5**

THE SEATTLE, WA, PUBLIC LIBRARY

The Seattle Public Library is available at www.spl.org. This large library is considered to be one of the best libraries in the Pacific Northwest. Being from this area, it has a significantly high tech flavor in its many offerings.

1. Computer Database

This database features articles about computers and technology, with a concentration on companies in the Pacific North West. **Rating=4**

2. Culture Grams Online

This database features country reports that deliver an insider's perspective on daily life and culture, including the history, customs, and lifestyles of the world's people. **Rating=3.5**

3. Digital Sanborn Maps

This database features historic detailed maps, showing street and building foot prints, for Seattle 1884-1951, other Puget Sound Cities, and cities of the entire United States. **Rating=4.5**

4. Legal Trac

This site features articles in Law Reviews and journals, especially law and bar association journals and legal newspapers. **Rating=4.5**

5. Safari Books Online

This site allows users to access e-books on computing, databases, programming, Web design and more. This collection includes titles published by O'Reilly for the three most current years. Any e-books that are accessed can be read while you are online. **Rating=4**

6. Ulrichs Periodical Directory

Complete information on over 250,000 periodicals. **Rating=3.5**

7. Washington State News Stand

This database has newspaper coverage from over 18 Washington State newspapers, including the Tacoma News Tribune from 1993, Puget Sound Business Journal 1999 to 2004, Seattle Host Intelligentsia, 1990-Current, and the Seattle Times from 1984 to Current. **Rating=4**

8. Press Display

This database allows users access to hundreds of today's U.S. and International Newspapers, in thirty five languages. These newspapers are available in a full color, full page format, with an archive of sixty days available. **Rating=4.5**

THE DENVER, CO, PUBLIC LIBRARY

The Denver Public Library online is available at www.denverlibrary.org. This library serves the greater Denver area and has some interesting regional resources that are unique to this library. The Denver Public Library features the following databases:

9. America's Newspapers

This database searches the full text of the Denver Post, the Denver Rocky Mountain News, The Daily Camera, the Fort Collins Coloradian, and other selected Colorado newspapers. **Rating=4**

10. America's Obituaries and Death Notices

This unusual site allows you to search by name of deceased or keyword, in a group of newspapers, including the Denver Post and the Rocky Mountain News. **Rating=3**

11. Morning Star

This well known database researches stocks, but is better known as a researcher of Mutual Funds. This highly respected Database allows identification of stocks, bonds, and mutual funds that meet your criteria, along with Morning Star opinions, as well as the creation of a customizable sample portfolio to see how it would work for your investment goals. **Rating=4.5**

12. Rosetta Stone

This database allows users to practice their English, Spanish, French, or other language skills. This resource is an excellent database for those individuals who are learning any of the languages offered by Rosetta Stone, or the person who just wants to improve their current skills. **Rating=4**

13. Smithsonian Global Sound

This unusual database allows users to listen to folk, blues, jazz, and spoken word recordings online, from Smithsonian folkways recordings, or other audio collections. This is a most unique database. **Rating=4.5**

14. Value Line Investment Survey

This renowned investment survey is one of the original surveys that rated stocks. In this survey, you may find company and industry rankings, forecast and statistics, as well as information and advice on over 1700 stocks, the stock market, and the economy. Highly recommended. **Rating=5**

In the prior parts of this chapter, we have primarily examined public libraries, their diversified offerings, and how we can make use of them. Many libraries, both at the public and at the university level, offer a database known as "Ebrary." This database fills an important gap in the coverage of other databases typically offered by other library systems.

EBRARY E-BOOK COLLECTION

1. Ebrary

Ebrary is a growing e-Book collection that spans all academic subject areas. The amount of books available on Ebrary is dependent upon the subscription of the library system that offers it. The top of the line version of Ebrary is called Academic Complete, which spans the following subject areas: Business Marketing and Economics, Computers and Information Technology, Education, Engineering, and Technology, Health and Medical, Clinical Sciences, History and Humanities, Life and Physical Science, and Social and Behavioral Science.

In order to use Ebrary, you must go through a seven step process. The first step is to download the Ebrary reader. Second, a personal bookshelf is then created to see highlights, notes and bookmarks. Thirdly, you can conduct a simple or advanced search by keyword, full text, publisher, or author, or you may use Boolean searches. The fourth step is clicking on a book jacket to open the book. Fifth, once the book has been found, you may then navigate through each occurrence of your search term, flip through pages, or go to specific page numbers. Sixth, an extremely valuable resource comes into play at this time. You may use INFOTOOLS to link to more information in the library or on the Web. Finally, the seventh step allows users to copy and print with automatic citations which include a URL Hyperlink back to the source.

In addition, Ebrary lets you know about newer editions of books published by major publishers. But there are some limitations to the service. You may read the entire book online, however, you my not print out a copy of the book in its entirety. There are also limitations of the number of pages that you may print and copy. Some publishers may also have limitations of the number of pages that can be viewed. Even with these serious limitations, Ebrary is a worthwhile research database for books. **Rating=5**

COLLEGE LIBRARY DATABASES

2. College Libraries

Another potential source of free information may be a college library. Many people either work for a college, or currently attend a college. As a rule, college library offerings somewhat differ from college to college and depend upon the nature and location of the college. However, as a general rule, colleges share many of the databases with general library systems. Most colleges do subscribe to a database that is unavailable to most traditional library systems in the country. This database is the LexisNexis Academic Search. This database is a somewhat stripped down version of the commercial LexisNexis database, which is very expensive to subscribe to. LexisNexis Academic allows for: news searches, quick news searches, getting a case by citation or party name, getting company information, as well as getting academic search results on a number of topics such as: news, business, legal research, medical, and reference. In my opinion, despite the excellent "buzz" on this database, I have found it cumbersome and difficult to use. However, despite these shortcomings, Lexis-Nexis Academic does deliver good search results. **Rating=3**

Upon conclusion of this chapter, I thought it important to mention a superior database that operates as an online library of books and journals, known as Questia.

QUESTIA ONLINE LIBRARY OF BOOKS AND JOURNALS

1. Questia, www.questia.com

This database is one of only a handful of databases that I will recommend that is a pay site. The cost of this database, $100.00 a year, is truly minimal in comparison to its capabilities. Questia is a one of a kind source of books, and other invisible Web based data. Questia has in its repository, more than 65,000 books on a variety of subjects ranging from: Business and Liberal Arts to Science and Technology. You may search the library either by phrase, which MUST be put in quotes to get an exact result, or by keyword. Once the search is invoked, you may look for books, journals, magazines, newspapers, encyclopedias, and research topics that are related to your search.

When a search is completed on Questia the results are displayed as a numerical quantity of books, articles, journals, magazines, newspapers, and encyclopedias. Any of these items may be clicked on and a full text result is then displayed. Questia also has the feature of adding any or all results to a personal online bookshelf, which maybe examined and printed out at any time. As far as the books go that can be searched by Questia, most of them are either older books from major publishers, or newer books by small to intermediate size publishers. It appears that most major publishers do not want their latest books placed on Questia. However, this limitation is not a barrier for the smaller publishers. Once a book is clicked on, users may examine the book by either chapter, the placement of search terms within the book, or view the book in its entirety. The book may be added to your bookshelf along with any of the results from your search. I have personally found the power of Questia to be amazing. Additionally, Questia has the ability to conduct searches from Middle School to Ph.d. levels. It is even possible to run an entire college level course solely using Questia as a substitute for a textbook. The students appreciate the value of the service, as well as the advantage of having a dynamic, updated source, instead of a static book. I highly recommend that any reader of this book who is serious about research purchase a subscription to Questia. **Rating=5**

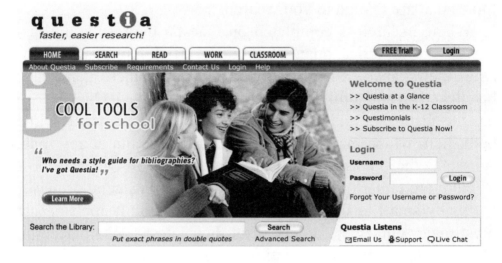

The following services also enable users to access books on the Web and are noteworthy.

SERVICES THAT ACCESS BOOKS ONLINE

2. Online Books, http://digital.library.upenn.edu/books

This excellent database lists over 25,000 free books on the Web, which are searchable by title, author, or subject. Most of the available books are full text. This is a recommended database. **Rating=3.5**

3. Google Book Search, http://books.google.com/googleprint/librry.html

It appears that many libraries are attempting to digitize their book collections (the New York City Public Library is the main one) and Google book search is attempting to cash in on this trend by creating a clearing house for this information.

It appears that only a small fraction of the books listed in this project are fully searchable. Many others are only searchable through sample pages, and snippet views, which give a few sentences and information about the book. In my opinion, other services, such as Questia are much stronger and should be used before using Google book Search. **Rating=3**

4. Booksearch, http://kokogiak.com/booksearch

This stark but extremely useful search tool allows the user to search inside books from three available book search engines: a9.com, Google Booksearch, and MSN live search. I have found this search to be quite useful. **Rating=4**

As we have seen throughout this chapter, there is a tremendous amount of free, commercial quality information available through your local public library systems. Certainly, considering the amount of databases that are available, there is something at your local public library that will serve the needs of every researcher. The value of some of the library offerings, particularly at the larger libraries, may total over $50,000 if purchased individually.

It is incredible that in these times of the digital information revolution, there is little, if any, real effort on behalf of the libraries to advertise their electronic services to the public. I hope that this chapter will motivate and encourage all readers to go to their local public libraries, get at least one new library card, and USE all of the available services to their fullest extent possible! Once you have your library card you can access these valuable databases from anywhere in the world.

CHAPTER 7:
NEWS, WEATHER, AND OTHER RELATED INFORMATION SOURCES ON THE WEB

Adlersparre

When a user goes on the Internet, there is a plethora of different types of information that they can retrieve and use. As stated in other chapters, the Web is full of a tremendously diverse amount of information that may be useful to an individual or a business. One of the more developed and interesting functions of the Internet is the ability to provide news, weather, and related information. Within these categories, there are vastly complex networks of detailed information on these popular topics. The problem for the user is not How to get this information, but rather, Where to get the data from as there are an endless amount of sites that offer this type of information.

In this chapter, I will highlight what I believe are the best, most popular, and most useful sites within these categories.

WEATHER INFORMATION SOURCES

1. The National Weather Service, www.weather.gov

This excellent and informative site is actually the information provider for all of your local weather information. This site has tabs for: warnings and forecasts, geographical forecasts, national maps, radar, rivers, air quality, satellite imagery, and climate. Below these tabs there is a map of the United States, showing all of the current weather warnings, with the ability to zoom in on any local area. Below the map there are links to enable users to place the map in a 12 hour loop (the last 12 hours, replayed for users), a 24 hour loop, or in high resolution. On the left hand part of the site, there are links to warnings, local forecasts by city and state, observations, forecast models, and climate and weather safety. On the top of the page is the ability to search the entire site. I have personally found this site to be an excellent source of weather information. **Rating=4.5**

2. The National Oceanic and Atmospheric Administration (NOAA), www.noaa.gov

This site is a much broader and more science oriented version then the www.weather.gov site. This site features long range weather forecasts from the NOAA climate prediction center and other weather related news. On the left side of the page, you may search the entire site, today's weather, global earth observations, storm watch, graphical weather maps, and an image of the day. There is also a tremendous amount of information on NOAA itself with links to NOAA's different missions. On the bottom of the page, there are links to featured weather sites and clips of various stories that are related to NOAA. **Rating=4.5**

3. ACCUWeather.com, www.accuweather.com

This commercial weather information provider provides local news and weather stations with a great deal of their weather related content. This site features on the left side, current weather news, below that, weather videos and accu-weather solutions for different problems, a long range forecast, a global warming blog, and a photo gallery. In the center of the page, there is a current weather story with a video. Underneath that, a national weather map complete with radar, satellite maps, and temperature and rain information. This site also has the ability to project short and long term forecasts for any area of the nation. Accuweather also has available for download a weather forecasting tool, which is typically branded along with local information. **Rating=4**

4. The Weather Channel, www.weather.com

This well known weather prediction service has many features that are available in their Website, including: local and long range forecasts, special weather items and videos, weather stories, and other video content. There are links on this page to: In Season, Plan Ahead, Travel Smart, My Neighborhood, Stay Healthy, Around the Home, Get Out and Play, Maps, Video, News, TV, Mobile, Downloads, Education, Local Weather, and Current Events. This Website is among the most comprehensive and user friendly sites for weather on the Internet. In addition to all of this content, there is the ability to download a weather channel forecasting center on your computer that will give you detailed local area forecasts and warnings. **Rating=4**

5. Weather Bug, www.weatherbug.com

This lesser known, but still excellent service, comes in two varieties: either on the Web or by P.C. or MAC downloads. This service has a great deal of information available, including: weather previews, U.S. and World City weather, severe weather conditions, and a multitude of additional data, including available Podcasts, and RSS feeds. The real value of weather bug however, is in the MAC/P.D. download program. Once downloaded and used, this program provides detailed weather information at almost a micro level. Weather bug gets its data feed from a tremendous number of locally based forecasting centers, including schools and other locations. This makes the weather forecast seem as if it is coming from your own backyard. Once the PC/MAC program is downloaded and initialized, weather bug comes up with a drop down menu, based on your zip code, showing you all of the available weather stations, and their distance from your house. This is a wonderful feature, and truly localizes weather forecasting. **Rating=4**

6. The Weather Underground, www.wunderground.com

This is NOT a link to the radical group of the 1960s! Rather, it is a link to a very interesting weather service. On the top of the site, there are tabs to current information, forecasts, aviation, and model maps. On the current page, there is information on item such as: wind chill, heat index, humidity, radar, dew point, wind, and satellite. There are also links to fronts, snow depth, precipitation, UV forecasts, flu, and air quality. The fascinating feature of this database is that any of the aforementioned links may be projected onto a map of the United States. For example, if I choose Humidity, the map of the United States that is located at the page's center, would show the relative humidity of all the major locations in the Untied States. In addition, maps may be reduced, expanded, and animated over a period of time. In the center of the page, you may view current storm advisories anywhere in the world by country, state, or region. Below that is a detailed weather forecast for any city that you store in the system. Under this is a detailed United States weather summary, a moon phase list, some weather trivia, a weather planner for trips, and this day in weather history. This site appears to be a favorite among weather "junkies." **Rating=3.5**

7. UM Weather, http://cirrus.sprl.umich.edu/wxnet

This highly visited site is another weather junkie favorite. UM weather has been providing weather information on the Internet since 1994. UM weather provides access to thousands of forecasts, images, and the net's largest collection of weather links. It may be one of the most comprehensive and up to date weather information on the Web. UM weather is brought to you by the department of Atmospheric, Oceanic, and Space Science at the University of Michigan. This weather site is packed with interesting links. On the top of the page there are tabs to: forecasts, maps, models, radar, satellite maps, skiing, weather software, travel, tropical, weather cams, and weathers sites. Many of these links are extremely interesting and useful, including the weather cam site, which has daily, live pictures of weather conditions at over 700 locations around North America. The link to weather software is, to my knowledge, the Internet's sole weather software archive that allows access to over 24 of the best weather applications for MACs and PCs. This site has been visited around 700,000,000 times and has received awards from many prestigious Web rating organizations. I personally recommend this site, and use it quite often. **Rating=4**

8. Find Local Weather, www.findlocalweather.com

This relatively obscure weather site provides some very interesting information to users. On the top of the site, there are links to a detailed local weather forecast, weather forecast maps, and other services. On the left side of the site, there are some interesting links, such as Airport weather, other areas of the world, a flight tracker, and currency converter. On the right side of the page, there is an area for weather forecasts and current conditions for any area throughout the world, including a current area satellite map. These maps may be modified to include weather, temperatures, humidity and or pressure. On the bottom of the page, there are links to CBS News, U.S. and World News, and CBS Top Sports News. Although this site, in my opinion, is not as comprehensive as some of the other sites mentioned, it is still worth a look due to its interesting attempt to merge weather and news information. **Rating=3**

I am often asked where on the Internet people can find a good source of news. The value of these sites is the ability to either present many news items simultaneously, or to act as clipping or other such news services that enhance users' ability to sift through the mountains of available news data. I will begin this portion of the chapter with a discussion of news aggregators, followed by general news services, and news wires, then with a discussion of Blogs and RSS.

THE BEST SOURCES OF NEWS

A News Aggregator is a site that filters news feeds and data from a large number of outside sources and then presents it all in an easy to read format. As a person who is both a "weather junkie" and a "news junkie," I believe that the ability to master news related information is perhaps one of the most important skills that a researcher may acquire.

Obviously, due to space limitations I could not include all the available news aggregators in this book, but this is a representative sample.

LEADING NEWS AGGREGATORS

1. Topix, www.topix.net

This unique, independent news aggregator features superior content in a number of areas. On the top of the start up page, there are tabs to: news front page, forums, blogs, local, U.S., World, business, sports, entertainment, off beat, real estate, classified, and browse all Topix. On the news front page, you may search all of Topix by keyword for over one year of Topix' archive data.

The News Front Page has links to Top Story, with comments, the latest news, local news, blogs, U.S., and world news with photos and comments. On the right side of the page, there is news from Business Week, and front page forums. Since Topics is an independent news aggregator, they draw content from a tremendous number of other sources, both national and regional in scope.

One cannot underestimate the relative value of topix.net due to its width and breadth of news coverage. This is a highly recommended site. **Rating=5**

2. NewsNose must be downloaded via www.download.com

This one of a kind program searches over 1,600 up to the minute news services, with a query mechanism that allows for search by one, two, or three conjoined terms. NewsNose gives users access to major print publications, online only editions, television stations and more, enabling queries by keyword, region, and content. Once NewsNose is used, and the results listed, you may click on the full text results, and print them as you see fit. You will however see a maximum of only 50 results in any given search. This is a wonderful resource and is an excellent addition to any researcher's bag of tricks. **Rating=5**

3. Individual.com, www.individual.com

This site is a superior news clipping service. Basically, a news clipping service is empowered to look for specific topics or content that users define, and "clips" of culled information form myriad sources. In the "old days" clipping services clipped to cut stories out of several newspapers, and delivered them to clients. In today's world, a clipping service "clips" from various news sources throughout the Internet. A commercial news clipping service may cost up to $5,000 a month. At individual.com, the service is totally free. An additional feature of individual.com is to have a simulated newspaper with your 'hits' on individual stories [by category] E-mailed to you in news paper format everyday. Individual.com searches based on a predefined list of categories that you may choose from in such areas as: My Topics, My Companies, and News Desks. Within these categories, there are also many subtopics related to the primary topics, and the ability to somewhat customize Individual.com to meet your needs. Any stories sent out by the newspaper which is produced by individual.com have a summary of the article, its source, and the time it was produced. Any article may be clicked on for full text printing. This is a wonderful service, and it is certainly priced right! It will be of great use to any person in need of filtered current news. **Rating=5**

4. AmphetaDesk, www.disobey.com/amphetadesk

AmphetaDesk is a free crossed platformed, open sourced syndicated news aggregator. This program is present on your desk top and downloads the latest news that interests you, displaying it in a quick and customizable Web page. AmphetaDesk has thousands of channels available, allowing for a tremendous degree of customization that meets any user's needs. **Rating=4**

5. Crayon.net, www.crayon.net

Crayon.net is a news aggregator that enables you to get unfiltered news from the Web's largest variety of sources. Once the sources are selected, and you are satisfied with the selection, Crayon will create a personal free news paper, and E-mail it to you on a continual basis. This site is also quite customizable, and is very useful for the news researcher of any age. **Rating=4**

6. Google Alerts, www.google.com/alerts

Google alerts are E-mail updates of the latest relevant Google results from the Web, news sources, etc. The alerts are based on your choice of query to topics. The alerts can be used to monitor a developing news story, keeping current on a specific industry, getting the latest in celebrity news or gossip or even keeping tabs on your favorite sports team. There are many services on the Internet that offer similar services as Google Alerts, however, they are usually restricted to content from their own providers. Google Alerts is not restricted as to the type of content it may use and this makes for a deeper more effective search result. Google Alerts are created by: search terms, the type of alert [from simple to comprehensive], how often the alert is received, and the E-mail you would like to receive it at. This site is an excellent news aggregator. **Rating=4.5**

7. News is Free, Your Personal News Portal, www.newsisfree. com

News is Free is an online news reader RSS Directory and news search engine, integrated into one interface. The basic search provided, such as the news search, RSS feeds, or the portals, are free. The News Portal keeps track of thousands of news sources and blogs on custom pages that can be created quite quickly. News is Free has a human edited directory that carries all the known sources that are necessary in order to conduct an effective search. Results of the search may be either E-mailed as alerts, headlines, or shared with another party. There are many different service offered by News is Free, including: news feeds that may be placed in a desk top aggregator, and news search that operates 24 hours a day, seven days a week in twenty five languages. News is Free derives their news and information from a great variety of sources that are very diverse in scope. **Rating=4**

8. The National FeedRoom, http://national.feedroom.com

This is a repository for the news feeds of several television stations, A.P., and other contributors. National Feed Room is broken down into topics such as tech, finance, and entertainment. Once these topics are clicked on, there are videos available that relate to each topic that may be viewed in their entirety from the National Feed room. Even though the available content on this site has dropped considerably, due to the fact that many contributors now host their own Websites, this site is still worth a visit. **Rating=3.5**

9. EUfeeds, www.eufeeds.eu

This Website, which is currently in Beta, carries the feeds of over 300 European newspapers, which are updated every twenty minute. For each nation that is selected, many newspapers are highlighted, along with their recent stories that may be displayed in their entirety. This is an excellent site, especially those interested in European News. **Rating=4.5**

10. News on Feeds, www.newsonfeeds.com/faq/aggregators

Although I have attempted to include some of the better news aggregators in this chapter, there are many more available that may meet the individual specialized needs of a reader. News On Feeds has a very comprehensive list of available news aggregators, with links, and this diversity of news aggregators should meet the needs of any reader. I encourage readers who are interested in News Aggregators to visit this site and test out any aggregators that cover your areas of interest. **Rating=3.5**

11. Rocketinfo, www.rocketnews.com

This news aggregator has tabs for news, Web logs {blogs}, audio and video on their opening page. Rocketinfo searches for audio or video/Pod cast news from thousands of sources and has access to over 30,000 continuously updated newsfeeds from around the world. News items are broken down into categories such as: Top stories, World, Business and Finance, technology, Entertainment, Health, Science, Sports, and Arts and Literature. Top stories may be sent out by xml feed, or you may download a reader. The RSS reader enables users to search, subscribe or read news information from Rocketinfo. This site appears to be quite comprehensive, and has a great deal of audio and video that are related to stories on the site. **Rating=4**

12. News Index, www.newsindex.com

This news search engine enables users to search over 50,000 current articles. This site's news search engine posted unusual results that were not readily available from American or Western search engines. **Rating=4**

LEADING NEWS WIRES

A news wire is produced by a news service for their customers and it contains proprietary content that is produced by that particular service. While there are many news wires on the net, I feel there are only two premiere services at this time that are worth writing about in this book.

1. The Associated Press (A.P.) News Wire, www.ap.org

This well known news wire has links to AP online video network, broadcasts, digitals, photos, international and other material from the Associated Press. In addition, AP hosts RSS, and Pod casts and this news wire may be searched directly from it's home site. This site is a worthwhile destination for those users who are interested in current and historical news events. **Rating=4**

2. The United Press International, www.upi.com

This is yet another well known news wire that has placed a vast amount of their content for free on the Web. The home site of UPI has links to: the most popular stories, top news, science, business, entertainment, sports, quirky reports, as well as news pictures, security, terrorism, religion and spirituality, consumer health daily, energy, international intelligence, health, and business. UPI also hosts a large video update section with videos that are available on many of the stories covered by UPI. Additionally, UPI hosts an RSS feed, and may be searched for stories covered in the last 90 days. Due to the comprehensive content available on the UPI Website, UPI.com is certainly worth a careful look by all who have an interest in the news. **Rating=3.5**

LEADING NEWSPAPERS

The next challenge for a researcher is to find content from newspapers around the world. It seems that recently, almost any major world newspaper publishes a large amount of their content on the Web. Even though this content may be searched by various methods or programs such as NewsNose [see above], it is always useful to get to the actual source of the information in order to correctly and accurately interpret its content. There are several thousand newspapers that transmit their content throughout the world. We will now delve into the details of the numerous search mechanisms that are available to find news content on individual newspaper sites.

1. Online Newspapers, www.onlinenewspapers.com

This site features drop down menus for each geographic area of the world, identifying where newspapers within that area are available online. For example, there are menus for North, South, and Central America, Asia Pacific, Africa, Asia, Europe, the Middle East and many others. **Rating=4**

2. World Wide Newspapers, www.newspapersonline.info

This interesting site allows for search of all nations alphabetically, a general search and a unique map search. This unique search functionality allows users to stretch out a standard Mercator map projection so they can see major cities and world capitals. Each city/capital may be clicked on, and all of the regional newspapers associated with each area are displayed. Due to the ease of search and the logical method of presentation, this is a very interesting and useful site. **Rating=4**

3. Newspapers.com, www.newspapers.com

This site features menus for a number of different search options for newspapers. On the top of the page, there is a link to display a U.S.A. map, which shows where newspapers may be found, a general search mechanism for U.S.A. newspapers, as well as International newspapers. On the left side of the page, there are links to the Top 10 and Top 100 newspapers. In the page's center there are drop down menus for all U.S. newspapers, U.S. daily and weekly newspapers, plus additional search options for African, Asia, Caribbean, Central American, European, United Kingdom, Middle Eastern, North America [other than U.S.A.], South American, South Pacific, and other world newspapers. On the bottom of the page, there are links to: college newspapers, publications, features, as well as television and radio stations. This site, enables users to search through over 10,000 newspapers.

Despite it's slightly awkward interface, this is a very useful site. **Rating=4**

4. The Interactive Museum, www.newseum.org

This useful site features headlines from more than 400 U.S. and International front pages. The pages are exhibited in alphabetical order, and almost all of them may be clicked on for further information. The ability to "see" the front pages of over 400 newspapers is a great feature, and makes searching this site quite enjoyable. There are also links on the top of the page to online exhibits and current features. This site is a favorite among my students due to its graphical interface and valuable timely information. **Rating=4.5**

5. The Internet Public Library Newspaper Area, www.ipl.org/div/news

The Internet public library is known as one of the best library sources available on the Internet. This site has, on the left hand side, tools that enter into the regular section of the Internet Public Library, such as subject collections, reading room, and ready reference. On the right side of the page, there is a list of major areas of the world, broken down into their individual nations, with sub links to newspapers within each area. For example, Central America has links to Belize, Costa Rica, Guatemala, Honduras, Nicaragua, Panama, and El Salvador. The entire library may be searched by the search bar that is available on the top of the page. **Rating=4.5**

6. Newspapers 24, www.newspapers24.com

On the left hand side of this site, there are links to major continents, countries A to Z, world's top 400 cities, the largest newspapers, and a search box to search the site. On the right side of the site, there are pictures from major cities around the world. On the bottom of the site, there is a countries A-Z drop down menu, with a list of languages that you can see content in.

This site searches over 12,000 online newspapers from around the world. **Rating=4**

7. World Newspapers and Magazines, www.world-newspapers.com

This search engine searches newspapers, magazines, and news sites in English, sorted by nation and region. On the left side of the page, there are categories and magazines that run the gamut from business and family to literature and sports, as well as many other categories. On the right side of the page, there are news stories of note, including: world news, business, Internet, sports, weather, a news photo, and other material. In the center of the page, are the major areas of the world, broken down by country. Any nation, once clicked on, will enable World Newspaper to then list the newspapers that are published in that geographic region. **Rating=4**

8. Online Newspapers, www.allyoucanread.com

This excellent Website has a large amount of information that is readily available to users. On the left side of the page there is an area that allows you to browse magazines, newspapers, and world news. Below that are features that include the Top 20 Magazines, the Top 10 by countries, and the Global 100 newspapers. Beneath that there is a link to free trade publications. In the center of the page, there is a small world map that you may click on to get newspapers by geographic area. Next, are newspapers in the most visited countries by site, which include the

United States, Canada, the United Kingdom, and Australia. The real value of this site is the next feature, which lists every nation in the world alphabetically. This means that you do not have be conversant with the regional area where a specific nation is, rather, you merely to know the name of the nation. This very useful feature makes this site extremely easy to use. Additionally, there is a search mechanism that allows you to search the entire site. Allyoucanread.com is a highly recommended site. **Rating=4.5**

9. Newz.info, www.newz.info

This simple, easy to use site has drop down menus for newspapers for all the major areas in the world. Additionally, all of the nations in the world are listed alphabetically. **Rating=4**

10. Free Byte News Central, www.freebyte.com/news

This interesting site is known for its large amount of news links in various areas. Among the links are: News by country, online newspapers, columns, science and technology, news archives, newspaper directories, and a number of other links. I recommend this site due to its simplicity of use and the easy access to a wealth of information. **Rating=3.5**

11. U.S. News Archives on the Web, www.ibiblio.org/slanews/internet/archives.html

Many researchers, including myself, have to occasionally find older articles than those that are readily available on a newspaper's home Website. This handy site lists many newspapers by state, describing the dates of archival information, and the cost if any, as well as a link to retrieve the information, if you so desire. I have found this site extremely useful in finding information from"older" newspaper items. **Rating=4.5**

12. The Headline Spot can be found at www.headlinespot.com

This easy to use Website has links to almost every possible news category a user can think of. Among the links on the left side of the page are: news by media, region, subject, opinion, cool tools, and Fun Stuff. On the right side of the page, today's Top News Stories are listed. On the top of the page, there are drop down menus for news by city, by state, and by country. Below that there are more links to top news by both media type and subject. Among the media types covered are News Wires, Magazines, Television, radio, and of course, newspapers. Among the items covered in Top News by subject, are: financial, sports, technology, political, and travel news, among others. This site is quite easy to navigate and is recommended to those users who need links to various news related items. **Rating=4**

13. Refdesk Newspapers USA and Worldwide, www.refdesk.com/paper.htm

This interesting site comes courtesy of Refdesk, which is in itself a wonderful site for reference material. In this Website newspapers are listed by state: top 100 U.S. newspapers, search-able newspaper archives, and U.S. News Archives. For world newspapers, the major world regions are named with the nations in that area or region linked beneath them. Just beneath this, there are links to the top United States news organizations. Following this are the top world wide Websites for news. This excellent site is an easy to use resource for any news researcher. **Rating=4.5**

14. Small Town Newspapers, www.smalltownpapers.com

This unique site has coverage for over 250 small town news-papers that you can read free every week. Users may browse and search the scanned newspaper archive from 1865 up to the current edition – for free! This site fills the gaping lack of coverage in the area of obscure or small town newspapers. These types of newspapers are important, especially for genealogists looking for ancestry records, and for researchers looking for birth, wedding and obituary announcements. **Rating=4**

15. Paper of Record is available at www.paperofrecord.com

This wonderful and useful database provides a visual representation of many newspapers, going back several hundred years. Although most of the newspapers listed are Canadian in origin, many United States and Foreign newspapers are also represented. This resource is visually clear and pleasing, and the results are shown as a digital facsimile of the original newspaper pages, with search terms highlighted in yellow. There is a download quota of 250 pages a day, which is more than sufficient for almost all users. This site is highly recommended and a must have site, especially for those interested in Canadian News. **Rating=5**

In our current technologically advanced times, newsworthy items may findfind themselves in a number of different formats, some of which were unthought of just a few years ago. One of these new methods of news transmission is by video. It seems as if everyone has a video enabled cell phone, camcorder, or digital camera. In essence, everyone is turned into a potential news reporter. Because of this, the video related news industry has exploded in popularity. I will now highlight some of the better sites, in my opinion, to retrieve video related news items.

Video Related News Sites

1. Search Video, www.searchvideo.com

This site, which is related to AOL, is a top flight location for news related video items. There are tools for sorting and filtering videos. Top videos are listed immediately below that. Information is available on the top videos, including: the time it was added to the system, a thumbnail description, its category, and its distributor. Just below this are important links which can show additional details about the video, as well as more videos like the one that you are viewing. I have found this feature to be of especially high value. On the left side of the page, there are links to browse the top videos, refined by category, by channel, by tag, and by user. I find this site easy to use and very useful in identifying relevant news videos. **Rating=4**

2. You Tube, www.youtube.com

In my opinion, Youtube, despite its enormous popularity, is by itself, not truly an effective news related video service. It appears that most of the videos on this site are not newsworthy, but are instead vanity or promotional submissions from individuals and/or video producers. **Rating=2.5**

3. Google Video, www.video.google.com

This good video search engine features mostly entertainment value videos, but still has enough newsworthy items to be considered as a potential news video search engine. A free special player must be downloaded in order to view videos on this site. **Rating=4.5**

4. Yahoo Video, http://video.search.yahoo.com

Yahoo video is almost in the same category as Google video, with the exception of needing to download a program to read the videos. It is also very easy to publish videos onto this site. **Rating=4**

5. Media Channel: The Guide for Internet, Television, and Video, www.mediachannel.com

This interesting site has links to the different categories of videos that are available here. Among the categories handled are: business and entertainment videos, health, educational, live Web casts, news, people, politics, sports, travel, weather, and Web cams. Also included on this site are links to several television networks that broadcast over the internet. This is a very easy to use and valuable site, especially as it categorizes all of the videos that are available. It also has a comprehensive news related section. This is a recommended site. **Rating=4**

6. The Internet Archive, www.archive.org

This incredible site is a major repository for much of the old information that was available on the internet. That "information" covers many categories including: moving images, a live music archive, audio, and text related material. Additionally, there is a link to something called the "Way Back" machine, which endeavors to take you back to past Websites. This site is searchable by specific media type or by all media types. There are many newsworthy items, past and present, that are available. The site is a repository of an incredibly amount of information. Among the more interesting material available is a viewable archive of public domain movies, as well as older audio recordings. This site is a must have, and is highly recommended. **Rating=5**

As mentioned in another chapter, news items may be delivered by many different methods, including RSS and Blogs. Currently, many news items are delivered through these methods to users around the world. In this following section, I will discuss some of the better RSS and Blog services, and how they may be useful to individuals and groups who wish to broadcast news over the Internet.

LEADING RSS AND BLOG SITES

1. Newsplorer, www.newsplorer.com

This site allows you to syndicate, aggregate, and book mark news items all in one step. Newsplorer can send news straight to your desktop as it has unlimited channels and categories. Headlines may be bookmarked and read later. Bookmarks are integrated with the social book marking service called del.icio.us. This book marking service allows for the sharing of book marks between registered users. In addition, pop up windows display the latest news items as they are retrieved, and news items are refreshed continually. **Rating=4**

2. Pluck, www.pluck.com

This popular site enables Bloggers to syndicate their content on the Internet. The site also displays various Blogs, including those that are political and news related. **Rating=3**

3. Feedster, www.feedster.com

This site features newsworthy items that are either fed by Blog, news, or Podcast. Feedster also has a real time newsreader that is available through Real Networks at www.real.com. This site is quite comprehensive, and has billions of posts that are indexed and fully searchable. **Rating=3.5**

4. Blogbridge, www.blogbridge.com

Blogbridge is a Blog and feed aggregation solution that can be customized for the individual user. This is a free download that is Open Source in nature, and can be run on almost any system. Blogbridge produces blogbridge guides, which are basically detailed topic guides on numerous subjects. Blogbridge can find blogs on any topic available and has experts to help with descriptors of different topics available through the site. Blogbridge is a top of the line RSS reader. **Rating=3.5**

5. Awasu Personal Edition, www.awasu.com

Awasu Personal Edition is an RSS feed aggregator and news reader that can announce news items via sound or through an icon in the start up strip (aka a tray icon at the bottom of the screen), and through a pop-up notification balloon. Channels can be easily added to Awasu through the Awasu tray icon for fast access to headlines. Many news feeds may be used inside of Awasu including Google, and Feedster. Many plug-ins are also available that expand the ability of Awasu to operate. Awasu is considered an extremely powerful aggregator that lets you organize feeds into different categories that interest you. **Rating=3.5**

6. Syndic8, www.syndic8.com

This unusual and little known aggregator has some interesting and unique capabilities. Syndic8 has resident on its home system site RSS and Atom news feeds on a variety of topics. Syndic8 gathers syndicated news headlines, and has a readable master list of syndicated news content. There are complete statistics on every aspect of the site's content available, as well as reviews and pointers to syndicated tools and sites. Feeds may be searched by name or by category, and featured feeds are highlighted. Additionally, feeds are available from sources outside of this country, and ten random headlines are constantly listed. This site is quite interesting and is especially strong in the area of financial and business feeds. **Rating=4**

7. My News Bot, www.mynewsbot.com

This is a site that seems to be dedicated to "news junkies". There are various channels available featuring different news items, breaking news items, streaming news, and Blogs which are all powered by Google News, a highly respected news service. The quantity of news items available here are impressive, and there is a strong emphasis on financial news. **Rating=3.5**

8. Bloglines, www.bloglines.com

Bloglines is a Web based news reader that aggregates RSS feeds and E-mail news letters. No download of any software is necessary, so there are no compatibility issues with any systems. Bloglines let you clip and annotate individual news items so you can retrieve them at your own convenience. News clippings may also be published as a Blog in Bloglines. Bloglines is one of the few RSS feed readers that may be use by mobile devices. Bloglines can be accessed from anywhere with just a browser. A browser window can be installed to notify you about new news items as they enter Bloglines. This is a fast, simple, and easy to use system for RSS feeds. **Rating=3.5**

9. FeedDemon, www.feeddemon.com.

FeedDemon has an interesting and facile approach to reading RSS feeds. FeedDemon is among the easiest RSS feed aggregators to configure and to use. FeedDemon has excellent tools and can retrieve information, on demand, from RSS feeds to meet your particular needs quite efficiently. **Rating=3.5**

10. NewzCrawler can be found at www.newzcrawler.com

NewzCrawler is a nifty RSS feed reader with an excellent user interface with many, many features and unusual items. NewzCrawler lets you post to Blogs, and search Blogs for related news items. NewzCrawler, like other news aggregators, lets you organize search categories, and use items just as if you were using your own E-mail. NewzCrawler, because of its excellent features and superior interface is a very easy to use RSS and news Feed Reader and is one of the best of its class. NewzCrawler is another recommended RSS and news feed reader. **Rating=3.5**

LEADING ONLINE NEWSPAPERS AND NEWS ORGANIZATIONS

I will now discuss some of the major newspapers and news organizations, and profile their importance.

1. USA Today, www.usatoday.com

This national daily newspaper has risen in popularity over the last decade. Their Website is a combination of hard news, and entertainment related material. On its homepage, USA Today is broken down into categories. These are: news, travel, money, sports, life, tech, and weather. Just below that there are interesting items such as: interactive media, the day in pictures, video and archives, among others. In comparison with its "hard news" competitors, USA Today, might seem 'light and airy', but this site still packs enough hard news that it merits consideration as a legitimate news service. **Rating=4**

2. CNN.com, www.cnn.com

This site is an extreme hard news service, providing coverage in many different categories. CNN specializes in video feeds of their stories, and in fact, has a pay service related to CNN.com, that offers even more videos, on different channels. CNN has links to tops stories, latest news, most popular stories, U.S., world, technology, entertainment, politics, law, health, science and space, travel, education, sports, and business. Each of these sub categories has a section page, video, and some have links to partners of CNN. Through this site, you may listen to CNN radio, or get E-mails and RSS of Podcasts on any of the major stories. Due to this site's comprehensive nature, it has become a favorite among hard news junkies. **Rating=4.5**

3. MSNBC's Home, www.MSNBC.msn.com

This site is not only the clearing house for the MSNBC cable network, but also for the entire NBC News Division. It is certainly well laid out and brimming with content in many different categories. On the left side of the opening page there are links to: video, U.S. News, Politics, World News, Business, Sports, Entertainment, Tech/Science, Health, Weather, Travel, Blogs, Local News, Newsweek, Multi Media, and Most Popular. Below that there are lighter offerings, with: games, gossip, horoscope, lottery, etc. On the top of the page, there are links to different MSNBC and NBC News related shows, such as "Dateline" and "Today." In the middle of the page, there are links to: In the news, "Newsweek," recommended stories, inside NBC.com, video, U.S. News, and a number of other categories. This site is very thorough in its handling of news content and video offerings. **Rating=4**

4. CBS News, www.cbsnews.com

CBS News homepage is one of the more striking homepages available in the news arena and is full of interesting content. CBS News actually enables users to view many of their news broadcasts after they are delivered to the public. There are links on the homepage to: U.S., World, politics, Sci-Tech, health, entertainment, business, opinions, strange news, and other content. In addition, there are links to many of the CBS News related broadcasts. Almost every news item profiled on the homepage has a video attached to it or some other interactive aid related to the story. There is also exclusive Web related content that is only available on the site. I believe this may be one of the better Websites for news on the Internet today. **Rating=4.5**

5. ABC News, http://abcnews.go.com

The ABC News homepage has links on the left side to U.S. and International, investigative, money, technology and science, health, entertainment, politics, ESPN Sports, travel, and local news and weather. It also has links to various news stories covered by ABC News. In the center of the page, each category listed has sub links with stories and related video. There are also links to: Top Headlines, Hot Topics, Investigative Reports, and ABC News Services which have RSS, Pod Casts, and E-mail alerts. In my opinion, ABC News has a very useful site. **Rating=4**

It is my belief that there is enough news and weather information on the Internet to satisfy the needs of even the most sophisticated user. The aforementioned sites are, in my opinion, among the best available for serious researchers, and those interested in the news.

I am sure that readers are well aware of the transient nature of some Websites. Therefore, there will always be sites that pop up and will be rated as the hottest thing on the Web-that week. The sites mentioned here, however, are established sites that can be counted on to provide a steady nurturing "diet" of essential information that is needed for your minimum daily requirement of knowledge!

CHAPTER 8:
BUSINESS, STOCK MARKET, AND PUBLIC INFORMATION ON THE WEB

As I've explained in prior chapters, the Internet has a tremendous amount of information available in many different and diverse categories. Among the more important and interesting categories are links to business, stock market, and public records information. There are many sites available that cover these areas. However, only a few of them merit consideration, as many are either pay sites or poorly conceived sites that are not as good as those selected and identified in this book.

One of the most difficult tasks for a researcher is finding public records on the Web. Of all the topics that exist on the Internet, one of the most requested areas by my students and friends is public records information. In this area, information is scattered across the entire Web, some of it in Government databases, some in private databases, and some not available at all (for privacy and legal reasons). It is an important skill to be able to find public records for a number of reasons. I will now list some of the best sites for locating public information.

LEADING ONLINE SITES FOR LOCATING PUBLIC INFORMATION

1. www.searchsystems.net

This large up to date and reliable directory of public records has unfortunately become a pay site, and thus is no longer free. The cost of this database is approximately $5.00 a month, which is not a tremendous sum, if a user needs this information. Searchsystems.net is broken down by: category of record, state, U.S. nationwide public records, U.S. Territories, Canadian Nationwide, Canada by province, Australia, Europe and world wide.

Searchsystems.net has information on business, corporate filings, property records, deeds, mortgages, criminal and civil court filings, inmates, offenders, births, deaths, marriages, unclaimed property, professional licenses, and much more. Searchsystems. net, however, is an aggregator of information. If a user wishes to get this information individually, or from other sources, it may be unnecessary to pay search systems.net. However, to be fair, Searchsystems.net is a time saver, and is well worth the $5.00 a month. **Rating=3.5**

2. BRB'S Free Resource Center, www.brbpub.com/pubrecsites.asp?h=1

BRB's free resource center is a comprehensive and searchable list of free public records sites, along with additional tools to locate sources for civil records, criminal records, driving, real estate records, public record venders, record retriever, legislation, and more. The material covered by BRB's free resource center is quite thorough and almost rivals the information available from searchsystems.net. If used correctly, BRB should achieve relatively similar results as search systems.net. However, a search may take more steps and time to conduct. A nice feature of BRB resource center is the ability to subscribe to a free monthly electronic news letter that reports on changes and current events affecting the public record industry. **Rating=4**

3. Free Law Links, www.freelawlinks.com

This site provides free public records and legal resources. Among the legal resources available on this site are: Law libraries online, legal research and resources, free legal advice, and most importantly, online legal forms. Free Law Links also has the ability to search each of the fifty states for pubic records. Additionally, Free Law Links has links to ancestry research, court and criminal records, corporate records, military records, property records online, birth, marriage and death records, among others. Public and criminal records are searchable by both name and state, which is also a useful feature. **Rating=4**

4. The Black Book Online, www.blackbookonline.info

This public records site has greater capabilities than others, and has some different features. Among the data available are: Social Security number validator, Federal data, state and local data, reverse look up, death records, skip trace, business, news search, non profit organizations, maps, and other searches. **Rating=4**

5. Federal Bureau of Prison's, www.bop.gov

This site has the location of Federal prisons and features an inmate finder for those users who may need this type of information. **Rating=3.5**

6. Zoom Info, www.zoominfo.com

This interesting search engine searches for people, companies, and the relationships between them. You may register to create a Zoominfo Web summary that describes you and the business that you are in. What this database does is search for individuals and where they are within companies. A reverse search is also possible for information about companies, products, and services. **Rating=4**

7. Argali White and Yellow, www.argali.com

This excellent program, which was discussed in detail in a prior chapter, allows users to search multiple telephone directories for a large amount of information, such as reverse search (search by telephone number rather than by name), reverse street search, toll free number, maps, area and zip codes, among other available data sets. Argali is a highly recommended site and a must for any serious researcher. **Rating= 5**

8. Reference USA

This database, which was discussed in the library based research section, has an uncanny ability to find information on both individuals and businesses. In fact, Reference USA is one of the best sources for finding information on privately held small businesses. This information is almost impossible to find from any other sources. For those individuals who are fortunate enough to have this database available through their library systems, they should definitely avail themselves of its information. I highly recommend this site. **Rating=5**

9. Yellowpages 411, www.411locate.com

This interesting database has links to the Yellow pages, the White pages, reverse look up, map directions, traffic update for major cities, public records search, and people pages. Although this database is nowhere as comprehensive as Argali or Reference USA, it is still worth using. **Rating=4**

10. The National Archives and Records Administration, www.archives.gov

This database is of a special interest to both genealogists and those who are interested in tracing their family history. This site has information on military service records and other data related to service with the United States Government. **Rating=4**

LEADING ONLINE BUSINESS & STOCK MARKET INFO SITES

The next area that we will be covering is the search for business and stock market information on the Web. There are certainly a large number of sites that cover these subjects available on the Internet. However, in this case, it appears to be Quantity over Quality as only a minority of these sites is of any value to the serious professional business user.

1. Business Daily Review, http://businessdailyreview.com

This comprehensive business related news service has links to a large number of other news related services that are also business oriented, and a part of the main stream media. Additionally, there is an archive search mechanism and columns for features and analysis, opinions and reviews, strategies and tactics. Even though the site has some annoying ads on it, it is a good starting point for researching business news. **Rating=4**

2. The London Financial Times, www.ft.com/markets

This well known financial newspaper is considered one of the best sources of business data in the world. This site has top news stories for world financial market news and data, an overview of the markets, the long view and stories from Wall Street, London, and the Asian markets. Additionally, there are stories on equities, capital markets, emerging markets, currencies and commodities. This is a highly recommended site for those interested in world financial data. **Rating=4.5**

3. Fierce Finance, www.fiercefinance.com

Fierce Finance is the finance industry's daily monitor, with news that covers the banking industry, asset management, capital markets, and SEC regulation. Fierce Finance has an E-mail alert for a quick daily briefing from an insider's perspective. The Fierce Finance home page has channels for different business related area such as: The banking industry, capital markets, hedge funds, mutual funds, private equity, SEC Rules and Regulations, Venture capital, as well as other areas. There is also functionality to search the entire site, as well as a news letter archive and a glossary of terms. In the center of the home page there is a link to an RSS Feed and top stories of the day, plus other stories that are of interest to the financial community. This is a recommended site for those users who have interest in the day to day functions of the financial industry. **Rating=4**

4. 1st Headlines Business News, www.1stheadlines.com/business

This excellent business news aggregator features news in a number of disciplines, but specializes in business. On the top portion of the site, there are tabs to the U.S. and the World, Business, Health, Lifestyles, Sports, Technology, and Weather. On the right side of the site, there are links to Major Stories, U.S. and the World, Politics, Space, News by State, News by Region, Sports, and other categories. There is a search mechanism that enables users to search headlines by different criteria. Below that, there are major business related news stories, along with links to the services that they originated from, and a description of the story. This site is highly recommended for those individuals interested in serious business related news. **Rating=3.5**

5. Investors Business Daily, www.investors.com.

In the investment field, there are two major newspapers that cover Wall Street. One of them is the very well known Wall Street Journal. Unfortunately, the Journal has most of its best content on its pay site. The other newspaper is Investors Business Daily, which has most of its content available for free. On the left side of the site, there are links to: News, research and analysis items, such as Today in IBD (Investors Business Daily), Daily stock analysis, Options, Media Center, Tech Center, IBD Newsletter, and other tools. Below that there are stock lists for the IBD 100, the Screen of the Day, and Stocks on the Move. Under that are links to how to invest, including a financial dictionary, investor's corner, and learning center. On the front page, there is an in the market section, stocks on the move, video and audio of stock market stories, daily stock analysis, news from Investors.com, breaking news stories and IBD Resources. All of these areas have many related stories beneath them. In my opinion, Investors.com is an excellent site, and certainly a reasonable alternative to the pay site of the Wall Street Journal. **Rating=4**

6. Business Information on the Web, http://ils.unc.edu/nclibs/davidson/busres.htm

This site is a comprehensive list of business information links organized by category. Among the categories listed are: Accounting, Banking, Bankruptcy, Company Information, Industry, Insurance, International Organizations, Dictionaries, General Business References, Economic and Trade, Marketing, Economic Statistics, Patents and Trademarks, Real Estate, Small Business, and Venture Capital. Considering the number of links available on this site, there must be something for everyone. Many of the links are quite useful to researchers of business information. **Rating=4**

7. SEC Info, www.secinfo.com

In the Government section of this book, I described in detail the SEC site available at www.sec.gov. The main attraction of that site is the link to the EDGAR system, which allows users to get information on publically traded securities. However, there is a problem with the use of the EDGAR system through the www.sec.gov site. The reports found on EDGAR are not broken down by category and tend to be extremely boring reading [even among professionals.] The EDGAR reports are presented in their original format, totally summarized or commented upon. I have found that unless you are a CPA or an SEC Attorney, you may have trouble reading and interpreting these reports. These problems are solved by using this free site that offers various categories of securities information from the SEC/EDGAR Database. On this Website, you may search by name, industry, business; SIC code, area code, topic, CIK, Accession Number, File Number, date, and other criteria. Filings are listed by most recent, today's, yesterday's, the day before, or tomorrow and thereafter. IPO's are also listed by both registrants and filings. Filings by type are also listed, including 10K and 10Q reports and registrations. When filings are placed on SECInfo.com, the filing is broken down by the following categories: Management, Financial, Transactions, and other categories. By using SECInfo.com, one does not have to read the entire document. Instead, one can hone in on just the portion of the document that they might need to read. This feature is an extreme time saver and eliminates some of the need for the "scavenger hunt" that exists on EDGAR. Other categories listed on SEC Info are: M and A deals, Tender offers, Insider trading, Institutional Ownership, Proxies, Late filing notices, Standard industrial classification codes (SIC), Registrants by location, and SEC Corrected and deleted information. Additionally, there are links to news and current reports (8K's). This site is an absolutely essential site for those individuals who monitor EDGAR reports, and it is highly recommended. **Rating=5**

8. www.secfilings.com

This free database allows you to track, discuss, and share sec filings, companies, and stock information. One of the most powerful features of SEC filings.com is the ability to create customizable filing alerts, which allow you to be notified when new filings of interest are available. Filing alerts may be subscribed to through either E-mail or RSS. The filing alerts page is easily accessible from a button on the top of the page. Secfilings.com is searchable by company name, ticker, or form type. This is a very good database, and it is highly recommended. **Rating=4**

9. EDGARscan, http://edgarscan.pwcglobal.com/servlets/edgarscan

EDGARscan, offered by Price, Waterhouse, and Coopers, is an interface to the EDGAR filing system. EDGARscan pulls filings from the SEC servers and parses them automatically to find key financial tables and normalized financials, placing them in a common format that is comparable across companies. Using Hyperlinks, users can go directly to specific sections of the filing, including the financial statements, foot notes, extracted financial data, and computed ratios. Tables showing company comparisons can be downloaded as Excel charts. EDGARscan is searchable by company name, SIC, or other criteria, and includes links to IPO's. **Rating=4**

10. Investor Fact Sheets, www.investorfactsheets.com

An investor fact sheet tells a company story, and provides an up to date snapshot of where a company is and where it is going. This makes it one of the more essential tools of investor communications. This service has a complete and up to date database of investor fact sheets available on the Internet. These sheets may be searched by: Company name, ticker symbol, exchange type, industry, sector, and alphabetically. Due to the unique nature of this site, it is strongly recommended. **Rating=4**

11. Financials.com, www.financials.com

This site has links to: basics, research, mutual funds. IPO's, annual reports, news, and other items. Current news releases are listed here along with links for quotes and other company data. **Rating=4**

12. Investor Calendar, www.investorcalendar.com

Investor calendar hosts an annual report service, which provides quick access to annual reports and other information on select companies. There are also links to European annual reports, and a precision E-mail alert system, which allows you to track funds and industries, companies, and Web cast corporate events. This site is searchable by either company name, alphabetically, or industry. **Rating=3.5**

13. Annual Report Service, www.annualreportservice.com

This service has one of the largest free directories of online annual reports on the Web. This site also has a link to the PRARS. com site. The PRARS site enables users to receive printed annual reports by U.S. Mail, free of charge. Annual report service is searchable by: Symbol, alphabetically, or by industry. There is also a link to pacesetters, which are pre-screened companies that meet strict criteria for potential investment. **Rating=3.5**

14. PR News Wire, www.companyreports.com

This well known news wire has links to: Today's News, Multi Media, Industry, Markets, International, as well as Investor news. Typically, PR News Wire distributes news for its clients, which are publically held companies. PR News Wire also has links to:

News by subject, Latest news, Hot Topics, Today's top stories, News by industry, and the latest video news. PR News Wire is searchable by either company, organization, keyword, advanced search or archive search. There is also an RSS feed available. **Rating=4**

15. Business Wire, http://home.businesswire.com

Business Wire is yet another leading resource for full text, breaking news releases, as well as multimedia and regulatory filings for companies and groups throughout the world. Registration, which is free, enables users to set up custom profiles. There are quick views available for: News by industry, Multi Media and Photos, News by subject and Language, and Featured news packages, as well as an RSS feed. **Rating=3.5**

16. Thomas Net, www.thomasnet.com

Thomas net includes content from Thomas Global Register and Thomas Regional. Thomas Global Register is the most complete and up to date directory of world wide industrial information from over 700,000 suppliers in eleven languages from 28 nations. This site is a comprehensive resource for industrial information, products, services, CAD Drawings, and more. The site may be searched by: product, service, company name, brand name, or the World Wide Web. Thomas Net has a list of categories that may be browsed for information regarding chemicals, hardware, metals, and metal products, among other categories. Thomas Net also has a business service center where you may get competitive quotes on services that are of interest to industrial users, such as: Medical and Dental Coverage, Equipment financing, and others. Thomas Net publishes an industrial market trend daily Blog, with a bi-monthly news letter, and an industrial marketer monthly news letter. This is an excellent resource for information on industrial companies and is highly recommended for individuals that are in need of this particular sort of information. **Rating=4.5**

17. Financial Week: The Newspaper of Corporate Finance, http://financialweek.com

This online version of a leading industry newspaper is subscribed to by corporate finance professionals. It typically has the latest financial news, exclusives, and special topics. **Rating=3.5**

18. Investment News: The Weekly Newspaper for Financial Advisors, www.investmentnews.com

This is yet another online version of a highly specialized newspaper for investment professionals and financial advisors. This site has an archive search, fund look up, news updates, current news headlines, At the Bell, reverse spin, short interest, and other categories. On the left side of the page, there are links to news beats, and different investment areas, departments, features, opinions and other links. The information in this publication is very specialized, however, it may be worth a look for those individuals who have a keen interest in investment news. **Rating=3.5**

19. Investopedia, www.investopedia.com

This site is different from other rather complex and targeted Websites as it is a basic investment Website. Investopedia is for those individuals who are just beginning in the market, or those who need to learn more about principles and jargon that is germane to the investment industry. Investopedia has an investment dictionary, articles, and test prep for the Series 7 Exam, tutorials, a stock simulator, and current stock quotes. There are links to: Today Inside Investopedia, and market commentary, as well as FAQ's. **Rating=4**

20. Investorwords: Investing Glossary, www.investorwords.com

This site has over 6,000 definitions and 20,000 links between terms that are searchable through the homepage, by either terms or alphabetically. Even though this is impressive, the real value of the site is in the Investorwords.com Term of the Day, which can be E-mailed to a subscriber upon request. **Rating=3**

21. Investor Links, www.investorlinks.com

This site has a financial directory, with useful links to services such as: advisories, commodities and futures, exchanges, quotes, stock talk, financial news, options, research and data, and stocks and bonds. **Rating=3.5**

22. Daily Stocks, www.dailystocks.com

This site is full of useful links for stock market information. Among the myriad links are: ticker based links, extended hours, detailed quotes, technical buy/sell signals, power ratings, free streaming real time quotes, ticker based tools, market snapshots, quotes and data, news letters, Daily Stock's Editor's Picks, Daily Stock News for real time traders, Trading time, keeping informed and break time. This very informative site has links to almost anything a trader will need, including newsletters, which may be subscribed to, and research reports. This site is highly recommended for professional users who are serious about the stock market. **Rating=4**

23. Big Charts, http://bigcharts.marketwatch.com

This extremely useful and comprehensive site allows users to create charts in almost any format they see fit to create. A user may create a chart by using basic, advanced, or interactive tools. Additionally, quotes, news, industries, markets, historical quotes, and Big reports are available. There are links to top news stories from the parent service, Market Watch, on the front page. I personally use Big Charts as my charting program of choice. This site is very highly recommended due to its comprehensive nature and ease of use. **Rating=5**

24. Stock Charts.com, http://stockcharts.com

This is yet another stock charting site which has customizable charting capability. The chart style may be chosen and there are links to a chart school which teaches users how to put together charts. There are also links to chart tools such as: Gallery view, Sharp Charts, Market Carpet, P & F charts, as well as different types of charts, such as public chart lists, breadth charts, dynamic yield curves, historical charts, and the rather risqué sounding Sharp Chart's Voyeur, among others. There is also a news letter available which keeps users informed about recent developments in charting. This site is recommended for those individuals who need to learn about charting. **Rating=4**

25. Briefing.com, www.briefing.com

This respected stock market update service enables users to receive E-mails several times a day with Briefing.com's description of current market developments. Additionally, on their home page, there are links to market analysis, stock market updates, headline hits, market view, bond market updates, taking stock, calendars, stock analysis, and perspectives. Briefing.com is a highly respected service, and this site, and its valuable custom E-mails are strongly recommended. **Rating=4**

27. Reuter's Investor, http://www.reuters.com

This top of the line news service is primarily for the use of fundamentalists who need detailed current information on the internal state of a company. Fundamentalists are concerned with the current conditions of a company, and not with the prior price movements. I myself, depend upon the site to conduct analysis on companies, especially since Reuter's covers many of the stocks in the smaller cap levels of NASDAQ and the Bulletin Board System. A potential user must register to get on the site. However, once they do, the amount of material available to them is dazzling. To find information on a company, you must first click on the left side of the page, then follow the link to stocks. Once the stock symbol is entered in, Reuter's analysis covers the following comprehensive items: overview, option quote, chats, profile and snapshot (especially useful for a quick view of a company's condition), press releases, financial highlights, ratios, financial statements, performance, shares charted (very hard to find for lower priced stocks), insider trading statistics, institutional holders, risk alerts, estimates, recommendations, analyst research, funds, ETFs, Options, commodities, bonds, and currencies. In addition, there are sections on ideas and screening, the ability to set up a customized portfolio, and video. In the center of the page, you may search by either company name or symbol for information such as a stock or bond overview. Also available are the top risk alerts, and the ability to browse U.S. companies by top movers, and hot lists. Reuter's Power Screener also can be found here and it screens stocks in the following categories: value, growth, quality, and sentiment, among other screening criteria. Reuter's

Investor is a must have site for all individuals who invest in the stock market, fundamentalists, or those who specialize in lower priced stocks. **Rating=5**

28. MSNmoney, http://moneycentral.msn.com/investor/home.asp.

This very useful site is almost as good, or even equal to the Reuter's Investors site. This site is currently the only known major site that offers free real time quotations to individuals. Like Reuter's Investor, MSN Money seems to be tilted toward the fundamentalist point of view. MSN Money has tabs on top of the page for home, news, banking, investing, planning, taxes, My Money, portfolio, RSS, loans, and insurance. Under the Investing home page, there are also links to: portfolio, markets, stocks, funds, ETF's, commentary, brokers, and video. On the left side of the page, there are tabs for current prices and graphs for the Dow, NASDAQ, and S & P. Below that are links to research stocks, research funds, get stock rating and see accounts. Next, there are links to portfolio manager, market (which include market report), news center, up and downgrades, lists and trends, IPO center, and more. Below that are stocks, with links to quotes, charts, and news, stock ratings, advisor FYI (an especially useful tool), earnings, research wizard, stock screener, expert picks, and more. Beneath the aforementioned, there are links to funds, with quotes, charts and news, ETFs, a fund directory, research wizard, 401K check and more. The stock and market section is especially useful in MSN Money. MSN Money also has on its front page, links to current stories and financial news. This site has included most of the content from the Market Watch.com site, and can be used in lieu of that site. MSN Money also requires free registration. However, in spite of this, it is one of the best stock research sites that is available for free on the Internet. Along with Reuter's Investor, it is a must have site. **Rating=5**

29. NASD Rules and Regulations, www.nasd.com/rulesregulation/index.htm

This site states the rules and regulation for the NASD. It has tabs for rules and regulation, regulatory reinforcement, educational programs, regulatory systems, arbitration and mediation, and investor information. On the left side of the site, there are links to firms and small firms, brokers, the NASD manual, rule filings, NASD statistics, and File a Tip, and others. This site only handles information for the NASD, however, there are other sites that cover other exchanges. The vast majority of all brokers and brokerage firms are quite honest, and rarely have complaints filed against them. However, there are always rogues out there who will conduct business on a dishonest basis. The NASD regulation site allows users to research the brokerage firm, and the broker, for their history of potential regulatory actions, so that the investor can see the past performance of particular individuals or companies. If something goes wrong, the investor may file a complaint and request arbitration through this site. I believe that it is extremely important for all investors to know their rights and be fully informed and protected regarding their investment advisors and investment decisions. **Rating=3**

30. CNNMoney, http://money.cnn.com

CNNMoney is the Internet home of not only its own site, but also of Fortune, Money, Business 2.0 and Fortune Small Business Magazines. CNNMoney.com offers an extremely graphic interface, with lots of video available. This site has coverage on: the latest stock market news, markets, technology, and jobs in the economy, personal finance, lifestyles, small business (one of the few sites that covers small busness) and real estate. This site is certainly worth a look, especially for those individuals who need content from the other sites related to CNNMoney.com. **Rating=4**

31. Bloomberg Investments, www.bloomberg.com

This site is very much like the cable TV channel from Bloomberg, full of current content with a very hard news bent. The site has a selection of more than 5,000 stories delivered daily on the Bloomberg professional service, which is subscribed to by most brokerage firms. The stories and data are delayed compared to those that appear on the Bloomberg Subscription service which costs more that $20,000 per year with a two year minimum contract. There are links on this site to quotes, charts, news, market data, investment tools, TV and radio, breaking news, audio and video reports, exclusive news analysis, and other items that are not related to the business world. Among the multi media tools available, are online links to the live TV broadcast from Bloomberg's TV cable channel, in multiple languages, Pod casts, Bloomberg radio, or Bloomberg wireless. This site is full of interesting content, but is nowhere as entertaining as some of the other sites. This is a great choice for those users who want hard investment news. **Rating=4**

32. U.S. Stock Market, http://usstockmarket.com/index.asp

This site operates as an aggregator for information from other sites, such as CBS Market Watch, CNNMoney News, CNBC stock news, Financial Times, and others. It has links to quotes and a detailed market overview as well as futures, funds, signals and sectors. **Rating=3.5**

33. Yahoo Finance, http://finance.yahoo.com

This interesting site is obviously associated with Yahoo.com. The site has links to: home, investing, news and opinions, retirement, banking and credit, loans, insurance, small business, and My Portfolio. You may also get quotes by symbol lookup or finance search. One of the strengths of Yahoo Finance is their message board system which enables you to "talk" to other investors. There are also streaming quotes available, as well as excellent links to: stock research, financial news, bonds and options. There are also many relevant and interesting news items that are tailored to specific financial areas. This site is recommended for all investors, especially those who are interested in message boards to discuss their investments with other like minded persons. **Rating=4**

34. The home site of CNBC, www.cnbc.com

This site is the Web portion of the well known television investment service, CNBC. The site is extremely graphically intensive, as one would expect from a site that is based in a visual medium. The site has links to: News analysis, market and economy, investing tools, video, and CNBC-TV. Users may get current quotes, news and analysis, charts, and video through the search mechanism located at the top of the page. This site has links to exclusive video events, Blogs, streaming charts, market diaries, top stories, and latest headlines. **Rating=4**

I hope this analysis of sites of interest to investors and those who are interested in business, public information, and news related events have helped to enlighten and enrich you. As stated at the beginning of this chapter, there are a vast number of available sites that cover the areas highlighted here. I have presented what I believe to be the best and most useful Websites in each category. I hope that you will avail yourself of this information and profit from the knowledge.

CHAPTER 9:
INTERNATIONAL RESOURCES ON THE WEB

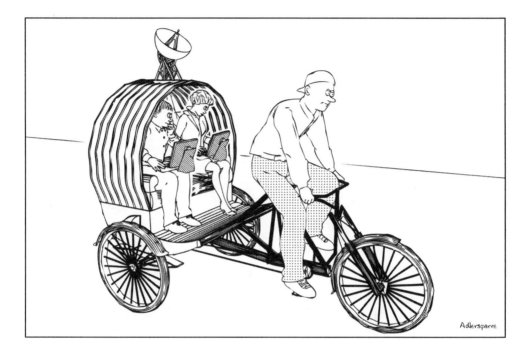

As stated in prior chapters, the Internet has a tremendous expanse of information available to users. One of the great assets of the Web is the international scope of its reach and resources. It can accurately be said that the Web covers all regions and cultures of the world. Given these facts, researchers face the dilemma of how to acquire and use the vast amount of valuable international information that is easily accessable. The uses of this internationally based information may vary greatly depending on the needs and goals of the researcher.

Many of my students are foreign immigrants who would like to keep in touch with their families back home. Other researchers may need to read some international news, or to evaluate a stock in a foreign country, or request information on a number of internationally related topics. In this chapter I will profile some of the most interesting and useful services for users of the Web's international information.

LEADING ONLINE SITES FOR INTERNATIONAL RESEARCH

1. Search Engine Colossus, www.searchenginecolossus.com

This useful search engine has a list of every country in the world in alphabetical order. Once a country is chosen, the major search engines in that nation are shown along with the languages the site is available in and a short description of the nature of the search engine. For example, if a user should select the country of Moldova seven search engines come up including Moldova. com in English, four versions of the ODP (open data project) in Romanian, English, Russian and French, Our Net in English, and Yahoo in English. Each of these search engines has detailed, locally based information that may not be available in another location on Moldova. Search Engine Colossus is a highly recommended site for both international researchers who are interested in a particular country, and immigrants who want to keep in touch with local developments in their home nation. **Rating=5**

2. BBC News Country Profiles, http://news.bbc.co.uk/2/hi/country_profiles/default.stm

This extremely useful resource is in fact even more comprehensive in scope than the CIA World Fact book (which was profiled in chapter 5 on U.S. Government Resources). Once a country is chosen, a map is displayed along with a summary, country overview, quick facts, leaders, media, and local media regulations, along with links to local newspapers, television stations, radio stations and news agencies. On the right side of the nations description page there is a national flag, audio clip of the national anthem of that nation, historical highlights and related BBC and Internet links that could be of interest to researchers on that nation. This comprehensive resource is an excellent source of country profile information. **Rating=5**

3. Language Resource Online, www.languageresourceonline. com/countries/countries_main.html

This database has an alphabetical list of over 280 countries, regions and territories. Any nation selected from this site can be profiled by either: spoken language, local news, CIA World Fact Book, travel resources or any combination of this information. This database is useful to users who concentrate on language related data or locally based news stories, however, in my opinion, this database is not as comprehensive or as useful as the BBC News Country Profiles or even the CIA World Fact Book. **Rating=4**

4. Nation Master, www.nationmaster.com/index.php

Nation Master is a massive central data source that compares nations. This site, as an information aggregator, uses data from such sources as the CIA World Fact Book, the UN, and others. Applying this information, it is relatively easy to generate maps and graphs using statistics on any possible category researchers request. Nation Master also has in its database profiles of individual countries, including their maps and flags, and the ability to create correlation reports and scatter plots to find relationships between variables. Nation Master also has in its database a fully integrated encyclopedia with over one million articles. The site has a toolbar and plug-in available which will work with most browsers and will allow users to get Nation Master's content on demand. On the Nation Master homepage there are links to: what's new, stats in the news, top stats and recent updates to Nation Master, as well as educational links and recent articles of interest to users. Nation Master is an easy to use, comprehensive, excellent, recommended database for international statistics. **Rating=5**

5. The IDB Summary of Demographic Data, www.census.gov/ipc/www/idbsum.html

This database, which is part of the U.S. Census Bureau, allows users to obtain summary demographic data and population pyramids for any nation. Responses are presented in both numeric and graphical formats. **Rating=4**

6. The World Bank Data and Statistics, http://web.worldbank.org (under the data and research link at the top of the startup page)

This useful service provides, under its data section, high quality national and international statistics and global statistical programs. In this area there are drop down menus for key statistics by country and data programs by category. In the research area, cross-country, cross-sector, thematic information from the World Bank's main research unit are available. In the prospects area there is information, analysis and advice on the world economy. Below this area there are links to key product series that are available from the World Bank, such as Policy Research Reports (PRRs) and Policy Research Working Papers. Next to that area are news and events and the ability to subscribe to a World Bank Research Newsletter, as well as links to site tools and other resources. This site is a very useful source of information for the researcher who specializes in internationally-based information. **Rating=4.5**

7. The U.S. Dept. of State, Country, Commercial Guides Index, www.state.gov/www/about_state/business/com_guides/index.html

Country Commercial Guides (CCG) is prepared annually by U.S. embassies with the assistance of several U.S. Governmental agencies. These reports present a comprehensive look at countries' commercial environments, using economic, political and market analysis. These reports, which are available through the year 2001, are quite comprehensive in scope and include items such as: executive summary, economic trends and outlook, political environment, marketing U.S. products and services, the leading sectors for U.S. exports and investments, trade regulations and standards, the investment climate, how to get trade and project financing, and business travel. There is also an appendix of data on the particular country, including such items as county data, the domestic economy, trade, investment statistics, U.S. and country contacts, market research and a trade event schedule. The reports generated on a particular country are quite comprehensive and are usually at least 40 pages long. This resource is yet another example of the excellent content that is available from the U.S. Government and is a recommended resource for international researchers. **Rating=4.5**

8. The U.S. Department of State Background Notes, www.state.gov/r/pa/ei/bgn

The background notes include facts about the land, people, history, Government, political conditions, economy and foreign relations of independent states, some dependencies, and areas of special sovereignty. The available background notes are linked by country. Once a link is used a background report on that country is generated. Typically, the background notes are comprehensive in scope and updated recently, but not quite as comprehensive as the country commercial guides. A typical background note can be about 10 pages in length. Since the commercial guides have not been updated since 2001 and the background notes have been recently updated, it is wise for a potential user to use both of these reports so that they can receive the most recent and timely updated data on a country. **Rating=4**

9. The Site-By-Site International Investment Portal and Research Center, www.site-by-site.com

This interesting site has information on world financial markets. On the left side of the site there are links to areas of the world, global equity research, prospective analysis and commentary, world stock exchanges, derivative exchanges, central banks, and other financial categories. On the right side of the site there is a list of G8 countries along with links to useful information on financial information, news items, and statistics that are related to that nation. There is also a world financial update with commodities prices, major indices, FOREX rates, world interest rates and other items of financial interest. Site-by-site.com also has available economic analysis and commentary, media highlights and an in depth discussion of technical information on world markets. This site is an important resource for information on world financial markets, especially since it is difficult to acquire information on many of those markets. **Rating=4**

10. The Spire Project: Country Profiles, http://spireproject.com/country.htm

This comprehensive aggregator of country profiles is an excellent source of links to country specific information in a number of diverse categories. Among the categories covered are: general information, travel reports, health reports, war and justice, economic profiles, further tools, library information, commercial databases, and a conclusion. Within these categories there are a number of links to excellent resources that can be of use to international researchers. **Rating=3.5**

11. The UN Cyberschoolbus Database, http://cyberschoolbus.un.org

This database, which is run by the United Nations, is intended primarily as an educational tool for middle and high school students. However, this database has links to some very useful information for international researchers. On the left side of the page, under resources, there are links to the Info Nation database and the Country at a Glance database. The Info Nation database allows users to contrast two or more countries to each other based on certain criteria. Info Nation has several criteria it uses for county comparisons. The general areas are population, economics, health, technology, and the environment. Once one of these general criteria is chosen, other sub categories for comparison purposes are displayed. For example, under technology the available criteria are motor vehicles, telephone lines, internet users, television receivers and newspaper circulation. I believe that it is very useful to see these comparisons between nations in a graphic format such as that presented by Info Nation. You may even print out the graphs in full color for comparison. The country at a glance database is, in my opinion, not as useful to international researchers as Info Nation and those users in need of country based data are better off using one of the other databases I listed in this chapter. On the plus side, there is a plethora of information on U.N. programs for children and for the Model U.N. Global Classroom programs. There are also in depth lesson plans, data, and instructions on U.N. issues and Millennium Development Goals, in the upper right hand quarter of the page. Be aware that with all of this information, this page may take added time to fully load. **Rating=4.5**

12. The United Nations Cartographic Section, www.un.org/depts/cartograhic/english/htmain.htm

This U.N. maintained Website has more than 100 general maps currently available. The maps are displayed in PDF format. There is a drop down menu available on the startup page which has a list of available regions and countries. The real value of this site, however, is a link to the U.N. map library which houses over 80,000 maps, some 3,000 atlases, gazetteers, travel guides, cartographic and geographic reference works, as well as digital cartographic products. This area is a useful resource and is beneficial to those international researchers who need access to map or cartographic data. **Rating=3**

13. International Monetary Fund Data and Statistics, www.imf.org/external/data.htm

The International Monetary Fund (IMF) publishes a range of data and statistics on IMF lending, exchange rates, economic, and other financial indicators. Manuals, guides and other material on statistical practices at the IMF, on member countries, and from the statistical community at large, are also available. Among the material available on the startup page are: the useful World Economic Outlook database, a 5 day trial to international financial statistics, joint BIS-IMF-OECD World Bank statistics on external debt, balance of payment, direction of trade, primary commodity prices, and a large amount of databases under the category of IMF financial data by topic, as well as data on a myriad of other topics related to activities at the IMF. This is a recommended database for those users who need high quality international statistical information. **Rating=3.5**

There are many internationally based resources that can be of value to a researcher. In the prior chapter I highlighted some primarily domestically oriented news services and news aggregators. I will now profile some news services that are primarily international in scope and coverage and, in my belief, are more appropriately placed in this chapter.

LEADING INTERNATIONAL NEWS SERVICES

1. The BBC World News Service, http://news.bbc.co.uk

This well known United Kingdom based global news service also operates as a TV news and radio broadcast network. On the top of the BBC news homepage there are tabs for home, news, sports, radio, TV, weather and languages. On the left side of the news homepage there are links to the areas of: Africa, Americas, Asia-Pacific, Europe, Middle East, South Asia, and UK, business, health, science/nature, technology and entertainment. Below this area are links to: have your say, in pictures, country profiles (which was discussed earlier in this chapter), special reports, programs, news feeds, sports, weather, on this day, and the editor's Blog. In the center of the homepage there are stories with pictures related to the latest news stories, features, views, analysis, as well as video and audio news, around the world now, features, views, and analysis. The BBC news network is a world class network and this site reflects the quality of their content and is highly recommended. **Rating=5**

2. Reuter's, http://today.reuters.com/news/home.aspx

This is yet another United Kingdom based world class news service that also operates as a newswire. On the left side of the homepage there are links to business, investing and news. These links are further broken down into subcategories such as: industries, companies, markets, stocks, pictures, video, blogs, and other links. In the center of the startup page there are stories and pictures related to world news, investing and other story categories. Reuter's is especially well known for their high quality coverage of world financial markets and other business coverage. There are also links on the homepage to an RSS feed and other news delivery alternatives. Reuter's is an excellent news service that is renowned for being fair in their views and coverage. This site is also recommended for those readers who are interested in international news, business or world financial markets coverage. **Rating=5**

3. EIN News the World News Monitor, www.einnews.com

Even though this site is technically a pay site there is still enough free content available to make a visit worthwhile. EIN News provides access to breaking news that is organized into regional U.S., state, and specialized topic sections. EIN News actively monitors over 25,000 news sources and other news related resources. A user of EIN news can select news by region or by category. Almost every nation in the world is covered and there are many different categories of news stories available along with news wires and in depth features that are related to that news category. This is an interesting and comprehensive world news site. **Rating=3.5**

4. CAROL - Company Annual Reports Online, www.carol.co.uk

This service provides company annual reports and the latest financial news. It is available at www.carol.co.uk. CAROL is an online service that provides links to the financial pages of listed companies in Europe and the United States. This is a valuable service since it is difficult to get company reports and financial news on foreign companies. I recommend this site for all investors who need annual reports and other information on foreign companies. **Rating=4**

5. International Investing, www.wall-street.com/foreign.html

This useful site has a number of links to international stock exchanges and other general links related to international investing. The available links are listed by region and include links to the stock exchanges that are in the area as well as other relevant information. **Rating=3.5**

6. Stock Markets of the World, www.escapeartist.com/stock/markets.htm

This Website has a list of stock markets of the world listed by country in alphabetical order. It also has international news reports that will be of interest to international investors. **Rating=4**

7. Wayp — The International White and Yellow Pages, www.wayp.com

One of the most interesting and difficult searches for a researcher is finding a phone number in a foreign country. This site solves the problem by listing areas by continent. Once a continent is selected a list of counties in that continent is shown along with links to the available White or Yellow Pages in that country. This site is a very useful invisible Web resource that can provide hard to find international phone numbers on both individuals and businesses in foreign nations. **Rating=4.5**

8. Numberway — The Free White Pages, www.numberway.com

This Website allows users to find both international White and Yellow Pages listings. Numberway has a list of continents along with links to the nations in this continental region. This site is similar to www.wayp.com and provides access to up-to-date international White and Yellow Pages listings which are available on the Web. **Rating=4.5**

9. Pressdisplay — Instant Access to 350 Newspapers from 65 Countries in 35 Languages, www.pressdisplay.com

This interesting site has a floating ticker-like display of newspaper front pages and headline stories which users can click on to get that local newspaper. On the left side of the site's homepage there are links to top stories, news, business, sports, entertainment, editorial and more, top newspapers, top reporters, top bloggers, an RSS feed, interactive radio, mobile radio, and titles by country. Pressdisplay also has the world in pictures with links to the papers that printed these items. Pressdisplay is an excellent source with a wealth of available information for international news researchers and is a recommended site. **Rating=4**

10. Worldpress.org — World News from World Newspapers, www.worldpress.org.

This world news site has links on the left side of its homepage to world news, with additional "sublinks" to front page Africa, Americas, Asia-Pacific, Europe, Middle East, as well as world blogs, world headlines, world newspapers, and E-mail updates along with RSS news feeds and other features. Worldpress has, among the Other Features section, a link to country maps and profiles with useful maps and information on all the nations of the world. Worldpress.org has an in the spotlight section with interesting links to stories of importance as well as latest breaking news stories that cover nations throughout the world. Worldpress.org is a site of interest for researchers who are in need of international news stories. **Rating=4**

11. WorldTop News Stories, www.worldtopnews.com

WorldTopNews.com has on its homepage links to world top video news resources worldwide, as well as world top news headlines (a very interesting link), news sources, technology news, financial news, entertainment news, sports news, and weather news. World Top News also has links to different world news organizations along with the top video news stories for each organization. This site is searchable by either news items or a Web search. World Top News appears to have some useful content and may be a site of interest for international news researchers. **Rating=3**

12. International News Sources, http://campus.murraystate. edu/academic/faculty/kevin.binfield/newssites.htm.

This site has a comprehensive list of news sources listed by area. Once an area is selected, such as Africa, this site then has a number of links to news sources that are present in that area along with the nation that they are associated with. This site also has links to unusual news related items such as "first nations," religious news, arts and letters multiple news links, translation tools, ethnic and alternative news, and general and breaking news. This location may be of interest to those researchers looking for links to especially unusual international news items. **Rating=3.5**

13. Babel Fish Translation, http://babelfish.altavista.com

There are many times when an international researcher may encounter a Website that has content in a foreign language. If this is the case it may become necessary to translate between the Website's language and your language. Babel Fish does a good job of machine translation on the fly by providing translation tools for a block of text or a Web page. For accuracy, however, double check the translation, as the accuracy rate is generally below 85% and some words do not translate correctly. Babel Fish has a large number of languages available for translation including: Spanish, English, Greek, Italian, Japanese, French, German and a number of others. Babel Fish is certainly a useful site for get-the-gist translations of both text and Web pages for researchers of international topics. **Rating=4**

14. Xanadu Translator, www.foreignword.com

This interesting site has word translation available for over 265 online dictionaries in 73 languages and supports text translation for 60 languages. This site even has a link to the NATO-RUSSIA military and political dictionary which had approximately 35,000 entries and to Eureka, a machine translation search engine for language and translation resources. Foreignword.com has tabs at the top of the page for tools, news, technology, translators, forums, software, as well as a search box which does translations of terms. There is also a link to the all-in-one translation wizard, Xanadu (a free download), which allows for Foreignword.com translation tools to be used in any PC directly from the desktop. This site is highly recommended due to the ease of use and the tremendous amount of readily available translation resources. **Rating=4.5**

It is obvious to serious researchers that considering the global nature of the Web, mastering the use of international resources is a vital skill to know. In this chapter, I have identified many resources that aid international researchers in their quest for information. This list is by no means complete and is presented to identify, in my opinion, the best resources currently available for international researchers on the Web.

CHAPTER 10:
SEARCH TOOLBARS AND OTHER USEFUL PROGRAMS

Adlersparre

In the prior chapters, I have highlighted methods of researching the Web's available databases to acquire a vast array of different types of information of use to readers. There are many other useful toolbars and programs available that can help researchers to conduct efficient searches. Once identified and properly used, effective search Websites can facilitate the hunt for desired information. In this chapter I will now describe what I believe are the best toolbars, search add-ons and other programs that can help researchers conduct efficient searches.

A toolbar is a program that is part of the Web browser (usually on top) that enables access to the useful functions available within that particular toolbar. Each different toolbar has some similarities and some unique functions that are provided in the architecture of that toolbar.

I will now describe some of my favorite toolbars along with a description of the functions that make them useful resources for internet researchers. Toolbars do, no matter how useful they are, take up space in the browser, and too many toolbars can make the usable area in your browser too small to effectively navigate. All the toolbars highlighted below use Internet Explorer (IE), unless otherwise stated.

LEADING TOOLBARS

1. Alexa, www.alexa.com

This useful toolbar provides information on the site you are visiting including traffic statistics and contact information. However, the most important information available from this site is links to sites that are similar to the one you are using at the time. Alexa uses Google Search which was discussed in a prior chapter and is not my search engine of choice.

Alexa is a recommended toolbar, and was recently made available for both Internet Explorer and Firefox based systems. **Rating=4.5**

2. Stumble Upon, www.stumbleupon.com

This toolbar allows users to channel surf the internet, get personalized recommendations according to interests, rate, review, and share what you find, and keep and share an online history of sites you visited. Stumble Upon also allows users to vote on sites visited and read reviews from other users on the sites. **Rating=3**

3. Wikisearch, en.wikipedia.org/wiki/toolbar

This toolbar allows users to conduct direct Wikipedia (users' edited encyclopedia) searches from within the Internet Explorer browser, without having to go directly to Wikipedia's homepage. **Rating=4**

4. Merriam Webster, www.m-w.com

This useful toolbar (especially for the spelling challenged like myself), allows users to highlight or insert a word in the search box and get a definition or Thesaurus search for that word. The functions of the Merriam Webster toolbar are also available from the right click menu upon request. The functions of the Merriam Webster toolbar are also available through Firefox via a search box plug-in, a right click search, a sidebar or a lookup button within the Firefox browser. A recommended, time saving toolbar. **Rating=4.5**

5. MapQuest, www.mapquest.com

This toolbar puts the MapQuest database of maps at users' fingertips at all times. In addition to having maps on demand, the MapQuest toolbar gives users one stop access to the MapQuest driving directions database, as well as the yellow pages, through an easy to use drop down menu. A recommended toolbar. **Rating=4**

6. UCMore, www.ucmore.com

UCMore sits on top of the browser screen, usually next to the browser's name, and does not take up additional room on the browser like a regular toolbar would. This toolbar, like Alexa, gives users sites that are similar to the site they are using at that time. I have found that results shown by UCMore are significantly more useful than those shown by other similiar toolbars. This is a toolbar for all serious internet researchers. **Rating=5**

7. Clusty, www.clusty.com/toolbar

This toolbar shows search and cluster results from the excellent Clusty search engine. The Clusty toolbar can also retrieve dictionary and encyclopedia definitions and any other Clusty function from any site on the Web. This toolbar also blocks pop-ups and is available for Firefox. This application is highly recommended for any serious internet researchers. **Rating=5**

8. Dogpile, www.dogpile.com

This useful toolbar combines Web search, white pages, yellow pages and a popup blocker, all in one toolbar. Additionally, the Dogpile toolbar has a customizable news ticker that delivers the latest news and information to users. Dogpile toolbar also has an RSS tool that can add RSS based tickers, blogs, news, and a search spy function that allows you to see what people are searching for in real time. This toolbar, which is located at the bottom of the browser page, also has a cursor available for search that allows users to search any word from within a Web page or Word document on demand by right clicking one's mouse. This is a recommended toolbar. **Rating=3.5**

9. Google, http://toolbar.google.com

The Google toolbar is available for both the IE and Firefox browsers. This toolbar has a search box, the ability to bookmark frequently visited pages, share Web pages with others, Web form filler, a spell checker for Webmail messages, a translation function and a pop-up blocker. Google is one of the most popular toolbars available and installs automatically with Google desktop. **Rating=3**

10. Yahoo Companion, http://toolbar.yahoo.com

The Yahoo companion toolbar is available for both IE and Firefox and helps protect a PC from spyware and other possible internet based threats with Norton security applications. This toolbar also has tabs that allow users to navigate to their open Web pages. Yahoo companion also allows users to check their Yahoo mail, use Yahoo messenger and other functions that are Yahoo based. **Rating=3.5**

11. Earthlink, www.earthlink.net/software/free/toolbar

This toolbar is available free for ALL users in both IE and Firefox toolbar versions. Among the features of this toolbar is a Scam Blocker function which helps protect users from online scams and other harmful schemes. By displaying a security rating for every Website visited, EarthLink toolbar also has a spyware scanner privacy tool, a cookie counter, a protection control center, a Web search box (defaults to Google search), a My EarthLink start page, and up to the minute news headlines in 11 categories. The EarthLink toolbar is by far the best toolbar available for security functions and based on this it is highly recommended for all users who are security conscious. **Rating=4.5**

12. Congoo Net Pass, www.congoo.com

This one-of-a-kind toolbar is available for IE and Firefox users. Congoo Net Pass, once subscribed to (for free), allows users to access selected commercial databases that change on a regular basis. This content would be quite expensive if purchased commercially. This toolbar is highly recommended for all serious internet researchers. **Rating=5**

13. Wizz RSS News Reader,
www.wizzcomputers.com/wizzrss.php

This toolbar only works with Firefox. It is an RSS and news aggregator. The Wizz toolbar is very easy to use and has a drag and drop quick view function for viewing chosen feeds. **Rating=4**

14. Reel New Media,
http://reelnewmedia.communitytoolbars.com

Reel New Media is available for both IE and Firefox and allows users to view live broadcasts from all over the world, including live TV, music, as well as movie and video broadcasts. This toolbar also has one click access to search sites such as Google, Yahoo, Dogpile, Wikipedia, Technorati, Shopping.com, Yahoo Finance, weather reports and a large quantity of other sites. The Reel New Media toolbar also has permanent links to a large number of worldwide news, entertainment, business and sports organizations, along with their available video feeds. This is an unusual, very useful and entertaining toolbar and is highly recommended, especially for those readers who want access to video content. **Rating=5**

15. Groowe, www.groowe.com

This toolbar is available for Firefox, IE and Yahoo Companion. Once this toolbar is installed users may customize it to include a list of preferred search engines and other sites. Once a search engine or site is chosen users will be able to perform all of the searches and other functions that this site supports. This creates a unique experience every time a different search engine or site is chosen. The Groowe search toolbar is a highly recommended toolbar. **Rating=4**

16. Answers.com, www.answers.com

Answers.com gives users free access to four million topics from over 100 dictionaries, encyclopedias and other sources. Once the 1-click Answers.com toolbar is downloaded it may be started up from within the browser, on the desktop, or by a right click of the mouse that can be used on any word in any program on the screen resulting in an instant, pop-up Answer Tip on any term users choose. The Answers.com toolbar is an extremely useful tool for any Internet researcher and is highly recommended. **Rating=4.5**

17. Fox News, www.infospace.com/info.foxnws/tbar

This toolbar has Web search capability, white and yellow pages search, a cursor search (right click on any word on a Web page), a news ticker (very useful feature), and other lookup tools such as horoscopes, maps, stock quotes, and weather forecasts. This is an extremely functional toolbar and is recommended for all researchers, especially those who are in need of a news ticker. **Rating=4**

18. AOL, http://downloads.channel.aol.com/toolbar

This useful toolbar provides quick access to AOL search, AOL or AIM E-mail, an RSS feed detect tool, news, the ability to share content with friends, investing, games, AOL radio, weather, and other content that is available on AOL. In my opinion, this toolbar is a must for anyone who is a member of AOL or needs access to AOL content. **Rating=4**

19. Windows Live, http://toolbar.live.com

This toolbar is offered by Microsoft and allows users to start a search from any Web page, protect against phishing scams and viruses, get instant previews of maps and weather from any Web page, and use Windows Desktop Search to find information on your PC. **Rating=2**

20. Web-radio, www.Web-radio.com

This nifty little toolbar allows users to listen to various radio stations, throughout the nation, that broadcast via the Web.

Stations are listed by category, and it is relatively easy to add new stations to your playlist. **Rating=4**

Readers should note that some search aids operate as BOTH a toolbar and a program. I have covered both types separately, so that readers can fully understand the capabilities of each, and utilize them to their utmost.

The next part of the chapter will be devoted to search aids, superior and useful downloadable programs, and certain miscellaneous Web pages that did not "fit" into the content of other chapters in this book. This list is by no means a complete listing as there are many more worthy programs available that were impossible to list due to space limitations. (These will be made available on my forthcoming Website.)

1. www.freebizmag.com

All users have to do to access this site is fill out a quick survey and freebizmag.com will find free business and other types of publications that meet your needs and interests. All of the referrals are always free of charge, and many are extremely interesting. **Rating=4**

2. Bpubs, the Business Publications Search Engine, www.bpubs.com

This useful search engine searches many business publications in several business categories, such as: Economics, Human Resources, Internet and E-commerce, SOHO and Small Business. Bpubs also has a directory of over 200 free subscriptions that users may apply for free business and trade publications. This is a highly useful site. **Rating=4**

3. www.sidestep.com

This travel aggregator searches multiple travel sites for the lowest fares on flights, cheapest hotels, as well as cars, vacation packages, and travel guides. There is also a download available that provides convenient access to sidestep from within the IE browser. This site is highly recommended. **Rating=4.5**

4. www.mail2web.com

One of the greatest problems that Internet users face is picking up their E-mail from locations out of their homes and offices. Most programs that accomplish this task only do this for one type of E-mail program. Mail2Web, however, can pick up E-mail from any computer domain, anywhere in the world, with no need for registration. Users has merely to put in their E-mail address and password, and retrieve their E-mail. Mail2Web.com works with most E-mail systems, and is a highly recommended site. **Rating=5**

5. Belarc Computer Inventory Program, www.belarc.com

This free download creates a complete inventory of all the programs resident on one's computer, along with a list of the versions of the programs, and license numbers, if available. Belarc also produces a complete inventory of all the hardware available on the system. This information is extremely valuable to have (print it out and file it!), especially if the computer fails, and is not properly backed up. This download is a highly recommended tool. **Rating=5**

6. Desktop Sidebar, www.desktopsidebar.com

Desktop Sidebar is an interesting information aggregator that grabs the content that you request from your computer and from the Internet. The result is a dynamic visual display that can be easily configured and controlled. Desktop Sidebar allows users to choose from a wide selection of information conduits called panels. Desktop Sidebar allows users to dock these panels to the edge of the screen, or arrange them anywhere on the desk top. All panels have a number of specific options available. The pre-installed panels include: News Room, Calendar, Tasks, Inbox, Notes, Performance, IM Messenger, Media Player, WinAmp, Volume Control Toolbar, Weather, Search Bar, Stocks, and Slideshow. This program is similar to an application that will be shipping with the new Vista Program. Desktop Sidebar is wholeheartedly recommended. **Rating=4.5**

7. Open Office, www.openoffice.org

This excellent program is almost an exact clone of Microsoft Office, except is looks a bit different. Open Office is fully compatible with all major office applications, and is completely free to use and download. In fact, this program is also almost a duplicate of the commercially sold Sun Office Program that is currently available as part of the Google software pack. I myself use Open Office at times due to its simplicity of use and easy to follow instructions. This program is highly recommended, especially since Microsoft Office has both a steep learning curve, and a steeper price! **Rating=5**

8. Netsnippets Free Edition, www.netsnippets.com/basic/index.htm

This free download allows users to collect text, images and links from anywhere and assemble them into one convenient location. Users may save and organize exactly what they need, including their own comments and notes, and they can share this information with friends. This is a recommended download. **Rating=4**

9. Copernic Desktop Search, www.copernic.com

This download allows users to search and to discover all the content that is available on their computer. What Copernic does so well is categorize and file all the information that is available on a computer's hard drives. It then becomes easy to use this program to efficiently search for any content that you may need on demand. Copernic has invisible Web capability, as well as a confidence rating of results. This makes it a highly recommended resource. **Rating=4.5**

10. Stickies, www.stickiesforwindows.com

This is one of those little-known yet indispensable programs that you must have. Basically, this program provides "Post It" like notes that you can stick or place anywhere on your desktop. You can customize, resize, as well as change the Post It's fonts and colors. A flag appears on your desktop reminding you where the stickies are in your computer. I have found this program to be very useful. Especially when I have to write myself a quick note on the fly. **Rating=4.5**

11. The Google Pack, www.google.com

As I have stated previously, I am not a great fan of Google's search engine. However, with the Google pack, it appears that Google is on to something. The components of Google pack include many programs that are available in other locations, such as Adobe Reader, Norton Security Scan, Spyware Dr. (Starter Edition), Skype, Real Player, and the previous mentioned Star Office. Among the proprietary contents components of Google Tool Bar for Internet Explorer are Mozilla Firefox with Google Toolbar, Google Talk (an IM Client), Google Pack Screen Saver, Google Desktop, which coordinates and updates the entire pack, and Google Earth, a global positioning program. All of these programs are free to users. I believe that Google Pack is a step in the right direction, but I think an even better idea would be to allow users to customize their own pack from an even broader selection of programs than are currently available. **Rating=4**

12. Esnips.com, www.esnips.com

This nifty little free program enables users to get 5GB of free storage on their server to upload and share files, photos and videos. From all the sites that provide storage, this is one of the easiest to use. Using Esnips, you may upload anything, share it with anyone, and tag and rediscover it on future visits. This site is highly recommended, and I have personally found it to be a life-saver when I needed temporary storage on the fly. **Rating=4.5**

13. Stumble Upon, any download service such as www.download.com will allow access to Stumble Upon

Stumble Upon can be found at any download site that handles freeware programs. It operates as both a tool bar and a program. Stumble Upon is not a search engine or even an Internet directory. It operates as a personalized browsing tool which matches your interest with the recommendations of other users, so that you may find relevant sites that match your needs. Stumble Upon uses member ratings to form opinions on other Website's quality. Clicking the Stumble button allows you to see sites recommended by other Web users who share your particular interests. This is a recommended site. **Rating=3**

14. DriverMax, www.innovative-sol.com/drivermax

DriverMax enables users to backup and reinstall all of those pesky Windows drivers. If you need to reinstall windows, all that you have to do is to install all the drivers from this backup without having to insert or search for the original driver CDs. There are many options in this program for the backup and installation of drivers. This is a highly recommended program. **Rating=5**

15. Windrivers.com: Your One Stop Source for Device Drivers, www.windrivers.com

This excellent source of tech support and drivers, offers free, unlimited access upon registration. Among the interesting areas of content are: Latest Driver Update that allows the location of current and out of date device drivers, as well as a DLL search, which explains everything you ever wanted to know about a DLL file, but were afraid to ask. Additionally, there is a weekly E-mail newsletter that gives advice in a number of areas. This is an excellent site, and is recommended. **Rating=4**

16. SIW System Information Tool, any download service such as www.download.com will allow access to SIW

This tool is available at any site that has the ability to download freeware programs. SIW is a stand alone tool that does not require installation. This sophisticated information source gathers detailed information about your system properties and settings. This data includes detail specifications for the CPU, network, TC/PIP, memory, hardware, users, network shares, and many other bits of information. This extremely useful tool is highly recommended. **Rating=5**

17. Feed43, http://feed43.com

This free online service converts any Web page to an RSS feed on the fly. This Web page can then be transmitted to other pages, or picked up by your favorite news aggregator. You may either create your own custom feed, or edit an already created feed. This is a highly recommended program. **Rating=4**

18. AOL.com, www.aol.com

The AOL.com program, which is advertiser supported, is now available for free (to anyone with a Broadband connection) and includes almost all of the content found in the older pay service. AOL.com may be one of the most comprehensive and useful of the free programs on the Internet today. The AOL service covers a wide range of content that includes: an excellent news service, consumer related sites such as shopping and autos, a large gaming section, travel, and excellent video search tools, as well as many other features. AOL excels in its social interaction areas such as forums and other meeting areas through its well known AOL messenger service, music, radio, its comprehensive entertainment and television sections (which include much classic older TV series and programs), and a free E-mail service. Other useful complimentary features offered by AOL include up to 5GB of free online storage offered by Xdrive, a free personal local phone number with voice, E-mail, and the ability to get almost unlimited storage on AOL Pictures, as well as a search that is powered by FullView that allows users to find text, audio and video on one page. Additionally, AOL offers free anti-virus and basic firewall protection (which are provided by McAfee) and other security tools through its Safety and Security center. This free protection is more than adequate for most computer systems. AOL has a large amount of useful content that should be of interest to a wide range of users. AOL.com is a highly recommended program especially for those users who use entertainment or social interaction based systems. **Rating=5**

19. Zone Alarm Free Firewall, www.zonelabs.com

This free firewall is a competitor to the free McAfee firewall that was describes earlier in this book. This stripped down firewall is still perfectly safe for the protection needs of the average user. I have found that Zone Alarm Free Firewall provides more than adequate protecting against most threats users might face. Please note that only one firewall may be installed at a time! This is a highly recommended program. **Rating=5**

20. BRB Publications: The Portal to the Public Record Industry, www.BRBPub.com

This is available at www.BRBPub.com. This useful site has both free and pay resources. Among the free resources available is a large listing of state, county, and city sites, as well as some Federal records content and information from some foreign sites. Even though it takes several steps to find free data here, the search is worth it. **Rating=4**

21. Property Shark, www.propertyshark.com

Even though only a few states are currently covered by Property Shark (Primarily the East and West Coast), this incredibly useful site is a vital resource for all current property owners, or prospective property owners. Once the address of a property is fed into the database, an incredible wealth of data is available for viewing, including anticipated current prices, mortgage data, an in-depth description of the property, and even a picture of the property. Recently, Property Shark has even included available foreclosures in there areas of coverage. This is a must have, top ten business site. **Rating=5**

22. Ehow, www.ehow.com

This fun site gives users step by step directions on how to do just about everything. Among recent topics covered were: how to treat back pain, how to rid your pet of fleas, and how to cope with flight delays and cancellations. On the left side of the page, you may browse all of the categories available on Ehow including such favorites as cars, electronics, Internet, Pets, travel, and other categories. Below that are the Top Ten Recent Ehow searches. This site is recommended. **Rating=4**

23. Instant Conference, www.instantconference.com

This useful site provides free teleconferencing services. The basic conferencing package is available for free and all that is necessary is for each participant to call a U.S. long distance number and then enter an access code. **Rating=3.5**

24. Scribus Open Source Desktop Publishing, www scribus.net

This excellent, professional level, full featured desktop publishing package is available as a free download and works with almost any operating system. Scribus is an excellent solution for most desktop publishing needs. It is highly Recommended. **Rating=5**

25. Adobe Photoshop Express, www.photoshop.com

This is a free, fully functional, stripped down version of the famous Adobe Photoshop program. Using this program, once you have taken pictures you may upload them to the Adobe site, and edit photos using many of the tools Photoshop is famous for. In addition, users may create albums and share photos with others. I found this program easy to use and very useful. Highly Recommended. **Rating=5**

26. IBM Lotus Symphony, www.ibm.com/lotus

Many "older" users remember Lotus 123 as being the spreadsheet of choice. However, since the glory days of Lotus it seems the brand has slipped into obscurity. It appears that with this new release Lotus may be returning again. This freely available office suite includes: IBM Lotus Symphony Documents, Presentations and, of course, Spreadsheets. This suite is being produced in Open Document Format which means that it will be compatible with many operating systems and tools, including Microsoft Office, and will more than likely remain free. Highly Recommended. **Rating=5**

CHAPTER 11:
WEB 2.0 AND THE FUTURE OF THE INTERNET

In this chapter, I have highlighted an assortment of toolbars and other programs available on the Internet that will enhance and enrich the users' experience. The suggested toolbars and programs cover a diverse group of topics, including Internet searching to E-mail use. I encourage all users of this book to closely examine these programs and utilize those that meet your unique needs.

THE FUTURE OF THE WEB

Now that you have gotten this far into the book, the next question you may logically ask is: "What is the future of the Internet and of Internet research?"

Given that the Internet is constantly evolving, improving and innovating, I will now look into my crystal ball and try to predict the future of the Internet and of Internet research.

Certainly, in the future Internet speed will continue to increase and the costs of a connection will continue to decrease. In fact, in the very near future, the dial up connection will become entirely obsolete and even DSL will be phased out. Soon almost ALL connections will be broadband based fast connections. The need for increased speed will be the fuel for connections that will support the ever increasing bandwidth needs of Web based video and gaming applications. Today, everywhere you click on the Web, there are either video clips (such as those on You Tube), video applications on news and weather sites, and even complete movies (available on services such as Vongo). These are in addition to the intense video gaming programs and a myriad of other applications that utilize fast broadband based content.

It seems that everyone is offering fast broadband content and companies in the cable, phone, satellite industry and other providers are all competing to offer fast broadband content at reasonable prices. The most interesting possibility for broadband in the future is the expansion of wi-fi services. These are, in essence, wireless signals that are transmitted over the air to a computer with a wireless card that acts as a receiver. This is the increasingly familiar and fast connection that many users access at airports and other locations. There is a current trend to offer this fast wi-fi based Internet connection for free in many locations. Currently, many corporate sponsors and even Government agencies are offering free broadband access to all users. Large cities such as San Francisco are already receiving (or will be receiving in the near future); free or low cost wi-fi access and the list of cities will continue to increase. I believe that in the future, most of the large cities in the U.S. will offer free wi-fi access to their residents. This will make most of the currently available connections obsolete and make broadband available to all users. This development may lead to a proliferation of new devices that access the Internet such as PDAs, cell phones, computer tablets and other devices that take advantage of wireless connections. Considering our always on the go telecommuting workforce, in the future I expect almost everyone will have devices that have remote connections to the Internet allowing users to remain connected from anywhere.

Another interesting trend that is beginning to take hold is the movement towards a single all-in-one device that incorporates the functions of several widely used currently available devices such as a television, computer, fax machine, printer, etc. This single device will operate as the nerve center of the future home and/or small business and would replace all of the many devices previously mentioned. This machine would naturally allow for a tight integration of content between the Internet and television. This type of integration is already available in a very rudimentary state on most satellite and digital cable based systems. With this all-in-one system it would be possible to connect to the Internet and receive interesting data or other supplementary information on any television content you are viewing. An example of this would be: while watching a movie it would be possible to connect to the Internet for a feature on the making of the movie, or while watching a game show it would be possible to actually participate in that game through your Internet connection. Additionally, I expect that there will be a tremendous increase in the need for specialized, on demand content that meets the individual needs of users, delivered via the Internet.

Another potential scenario for the use of the all in one device is a family who would wake up and receive a schedule for the day automatically downloaded to their PDAs, as well as a current updated newspaper that would be tailored to the individual needs of each family member. Such a device will also control the security and other functions of the house, such as environmental functions, without the need for human interaction. I would expect that this all-in-one device will become available in the near future.

A serious concern about the future of the Internet is the need for a secure system that is safe from unauthorized users. Everyone is familiar with the many dangers that are out there such as: scams, phishing, spyware, viruses, malware, identity theft and a myriad of other pitfalls. Many users are frightened and concerned when they use the Internet and have been victims of Internet-based crimes, and many others do not know how to secure their systems or deter intruders. In the future, I anticipate that there will be a powerful program that will provide both fully customizable solutions to one's Internet security and will be easy to use. This future Internet security program will more than likely be server based and customizable for the needs of each individual user. The most recent release of Windows Microsoft Vista is a step in the right direction in the areas of both Internet and system security. The new version of Internet Explorer (IE) release 7 has tools that increase both the usability and security of IE. Yet, even with the release of Vista and the new version of Internet Explorer, there is still a lot of work to be done to improve Internet security. This issue MUST be addressed in order to create user confidence in the especially vulnerable wi-fi systems, if the plan for the nationwide rollout of these systems is to succeed.

In the near future the Internet itself may be challenged to find enough "space" for all of the users. It appears that the capacity requirements of the Internet are increasing geometrically. In the near future the Internet will have to accommodate even more users with increasing demands for broadband based applications that require even more speed and more Internet space. Even today, at times it seems as if the Internet has reached its full capacity and has either slowed down or ground to a halt entirely due to the demands placed by users on servers and other equipment that keeps the Internet running. In the next few years it will be necessary to expand the capacity of cyberspace and the Internet so there will not be catastrophic failures that will cause both massive service interruptions, as well as a loss of confidence in the systems and the ISPs that are the backbone of the Internet.

The damage caused by a substantial disruption of the Internet would be almost unthinkable to personal, business, and government users. This potentially catastrophic situation must obviously be avoided. The future reliability of the Internet depends on our response to these potential infrastructure and security problems today.

Another interesting trend that has recently developed is the use of portable storage devices to allow users to have immediate access to a large amount of data at a low cost. These newer devices range from thumb drives, that can be carried or even worn by an individual, to large capacity portable hard drives and even SD memory that is commonplace in PDAs and other portable devices. Just a few years ago such devices were either too expensive to be practical or not available at all. Today almost everyone uses portable storage devices for a myriad of purposes such as MP3 players, cell phone storage, digital camera storage, game storage and personal file storage. I expect that these devices will play an important part in the Internet of the future since applications are being developed today that will make optimal use of these devices.

The next logical step in the evolution of the Internet will be the miniaturization of future devices, as well as the creation of more portable devices. These will almost certainly be wireless. Additionally, these devices will be like mini-computers with sophisticated color screens, advanced keyboards, and a generous amount of attached and removable memory.

Logically, a user may conclude that, "This device may be useful as a PDA or a cell phone, or even a Blackberry. But this small device cannot perform the functions that a business user would typically need." This problem appears to be solved by a new trend in software called Web 2.0. The developers of Web 2.0 believe that this software allows data to interact among several programs that are Web based, allowing this data to be exchanged and manipulated. It is my belief that there will be continued migration of programs to make them Web 2.0 based, which will lead to the future elimination of all home based computers, and their need for large amounts of dedicated file storage.

Web 2.0 applications are currently being developed and perfected. However, since this is a relatively new area of software development, the applications tend to be rudimentary, and rather simple in design. The most popular definition of Web 2.0 applications are those applications that are dependent on user content and interaction such as Wikipedia. I disagree with this definition and believe that Web 2.0 applications are those applications that are completely Web based including any storage requirements for saved content. It is my belief that in the very near future these applications will become as robust and as useful as their current desktop computer based brethren are.

I will now list several of the new, ground breaking future applications and their potential usefulness. As with most of these applications, there will be almost no storage necessary on the user's computer. These programs allow for data storage and other file storage on the systems that host them. A major concern I have at this time is regarding the safety and confidentiality of the data stored on the host computer. In order for Web 2.0 to be successful, data security is going to have to be a primary concern for both the host and the user. The other problem that is inherent with many Web 2.0 applications is that they are written in AJAX-A Synchronous Java Script and XML. The reasons for this are to make Web pages update more rapidly, and to exchange data with the servers behind the scenes. However, AJAX language cannot be seen by most search engines that do not support Java Script. It is because of this that most AJAX based, Web 2.0 applications are invisible Web in nature.

The development of Web 2.0 and AJAX has led to the spawning of a large number of applications that use this technology. As with all applications, many are good, some are bad, and some are even ugly. In this section I will sort out the best of a very new breed of embryonic applications.

THE BEST OF THE NEW APPLICATIONS
(These are unrated as they are evolving so rapidly that ranking would be inaccurate.)

1. The application that is most familiar to the majority of readers: Google Docs and Spread Sheet, http://docs.google.com

Google Docs and Spread Sheet are extremely simple, but useful word processor and spread sheet applications that allow for basic use of word processing and number crunching. It is certainly no substitute for a full powered program such as Microsoft's Word or Excel. In fact, Google Docs is not 100% Word capable and may cause problems for larger documents. And the spread sheets are not 100% Excel compatible either. However, when you are doing a quick, "down and dirty" document, while you are away from your main computer, this applications may turn out to be useful.

2. Think Free Office Online, www.thinkfree.com

This suite has a write and calc function that hides within your browser's menu bar and allows you to use keyboard shortcuts. Thinkfree also has a presentation module for creating Power Point compatible files that may be shared by using either Thinkfree mail, Google Gmail, Hotmail, or even Microsoft Outlook Express. Another feature in Thinkfree allows the user to view documents by right clicking a link to a document. Thinkfree has collaborative documentation capability where users can share there documentation with others. Thinkfree offers 1GB of free workspace on their server, and looks and acts a lot like Microsoft Office. In fact, Thinkfree is like Office 'Light', and, in my tests, was able to handle most Office documents with ease. Considering that this is a free application, the user has nothing to loose by trying it.

3. ZOHO Office Suite, www.zoho.com

Includes: a word processor, a spread sheet, project management software, presentation software, a database manager, reminders with notes, and an organizer. It also has groupware with calendar, an E-mail client and a myriad of other features. Feature wise, ZOHO Suite is much more in line with the higher powered Pay suites that users are accustomed to, such as Microsoft Office and Lotus Smart Suite. When I used ZOHO office, I found that it does a very good job on performing basic functions. However, as of this writing, there are very few advanced functions available. ZOHO writer works under Internet Explorer and Firefox. ZOHO gives you a free 1 gigabyte online library to store data that can be exported in almost every conceivable format. Personally, I like ZOHO Office, considering the plethora of features available and the generous amount of free online storage. Even though ZOHO office is a bit crude in its current form, I believe that in the future, ZOHO office will become the thoroughbred of Web 2.0 office suites. As such, it is highly recommended.

The next set of applications cover many miscellaneous online categories that will be of interest to a wide range of readers.

MISCELLANEOUS VALUABLE APPLICATIONS

1. RELENTACRM, www.relentacrm.com

RELENTACRM is a nifty little program that allows you to keep E-mail, contacts, and documents in one location, which, in turn, can also be shared by other users.

2. NENEST, www.nenest.com

This program allows users to create Internet software programs that support applications such as on line forms, surveys, storage, and Web notebooks.

3. METAGLOSSARY, www.metaglossary.com

METAGLOSSARY searches the entire Web for definitions of terms that the user requests.

4. PIPL, www.pipl.com

PIPL is an extremely interesting and comprehensive search engine. PIPL searches deep Web sources to find information on any individual that you request. I recently used PIPL, and I found this to be comprehensive and even scary at times in the detail that this personal search engine turned up! This is a MUST HAVE, HIGHLY RECOMMENDED PROGRAM.

5. DOHOP, www.dohop.com

DOHOP is a travel search engine that gives rather comprehensive results. DOHOP will allow the user to find low cost fairs on airlines, and multi-flight solutions, which include hidden cities.

6. ATLAS, www.atlas.com

ATLAS uses Mircosoft Virtual Earth, which, along with local search driving directions, also provides local information on events, movies, and other important and useful data. This site was very comprehensive in its results.

7. JOTT, www.jott.com

JOTT allows a user to have a designated phone number which the user can then utilize to dictate any message that they need to record. (The recording time is more than ample.) This oral message is then converted automatically to a digital text format and can be sent, by either text message or E-mail, to any person you designate.

8. FREEWEBS, www.freeWebs.com

FREEWEBS gives the user the tools required to create their own personal space on the Web. FREEWEB also includes a number of available templates, which you can use to customize this Web page.

9. CALENDARHUB, www.calendarhub.com

This well known program creates your own online calendar which may be customized.

10. SPONGECELL, www.spongecell.com

SPONGECELL is yet another on line calendar service that is loaded with features and highly interactive. SPONGECELL allows users to receive reminders on a cell phone, RSS, or other methods of notification. It also allows users to send and receive high volumes of E-mail for the promotion of events and for the receipt of RSVPs.

11. JOOPZ, www.joopz.com

JOOPZ is a Web based messaging service that allows texting over the Internet and two easy communications to any mobile phone, and back.

12. YUGMA, www.yugma.com

YUGMA is a free Web conferencing service that allows parties to connect over the Internet and to use any application or software that facilitates this connection.

13. LINKED IN, www.linkedin.com

This is a contact related, professional networking program. This program allows users to share knowledge, create relationships and connect with professional people with similar interests. There is also a section available for news that your colleagues may be reading. Recently, Linked In has added information on different companies and industries. Highly Recommended.

14. EBUDDY, www.ebuddy.com

This service allows users to securely log on to their preferred IM client without having to register or download any software. EBUDDY is available for all popular IM clients, such as MSN, Yahoo, AIM, and ICQ.

15. MINT, www.mint.com

Mint is a FREE online finance program. Mint connects securely with more than 5,000 financial institutions and allows users to plan an effective personal budget. Mint automatically retrieves and categorizes new transactions and keeps track of changes in the accounts you entered into the system and e-mails you with account alerts. You may track and even compare your spending patterns to others. A HIGHLY RECOMMENDED PROGRAM.

16. GIGATRIBE, www.gigatribe.com

This software allows you to share folders on your computer with anyone, anywhere, via the Internet connection.

17. SCANR, www.scanr.com

This interesting service enables you to capture information contained in any document using your mobile camera phone, or digital camera which scans photos into legible digital PDF files that may be sent by either E-mail or fax to any user. A very useful recommended program.

18. TAPE FAILURE, www.tapefailure.com

This site allows the individual to record an entire browsing session over the Internet and play it back again, or send it to any user.

19. PANDORA, www.pandora.com

PANDORA is a music discovery service that creates a music station to the unique taste of each user. All you have to do is to choose a song or artist, and PANDORA will trace and make available to you music of similar type to your original song or artist.

20. MEDIAFIRE, www.mediafire.com

This file sharing online application allows the user to send and to receive files that are very large and too cumbersome to be sent by other methods. Mediafire handles up to 100MB per file. I have found this to be more than adequate for most files.

21. AVVENU, www.avvenu.com

This nifty application allows users to access their home or office computer from anywhere in the world with any mobile device or computer. Then users may share the content with anyone using the Internet.

22. 411SYNC, www.411sync.com

This application allows the user to get information on their cell phone by many methods such as WAP, SMS, or E-mail.

23. PXN8, www.pxn8.com

This program is an on line photo editor to edit photos and to save the images either on the Internet or for use in other applications.

24. FLASH EARTH, www.flashearth.com

This useful program has the power of several satellite imagery programs combined into one interface. Programs such as Google Local, Windows Live Local, Yahoo Maps, Ask.com Maps and others are used and you may select the best image available from the available programs.

25. FARECAST, www.farecast.com

Farecast collects fare prices over time and uses algorithms to make a calculated guess when it may be time for fares to be reduced. An interesting and unique program.

26. WEB 2 RSS, www.Web2rss.com

This easy to use program converts any Website or page into a RSS document making it easy to receive updates in a feed reader to publish a page using a RSS syndicator.

27. ZOOMINFO, www.zoominfo.com

This valuable site helps users find useful information about people or companies on the Web. Zoominfo especially excels at company searches since it draws data from a variety of news services, filing sources and other online sources. This is a recommended site.

28. SIMPLY HIRED, www.simplyhired.com

Simply hired is a unique job search engine that not only provides conventional job listings but also provides unique job listings in areas such as dog friendly or working mother friendly companies.

29. MICROSOFT WINDOWS LIVE, www.windowslive.com

This excellent, FREE program allows users to access several useful tools that are available. They may access the MSN instant messenger, Hotmail, a photo gallery, MSN writer (which is similar to Writely and allows for quick blogging or publication of documents), spaces (a social networking area), events (a useful calendar), and Skydrive which allows the user 5 MB of free storage space. This is an excellent suite of programs and is highly recommended.

30. MICROSOFT VIRTUAL EARTH, www.microsoft.com/virtualearth

This excellent satellite mapping and searching program allows for both two dimensional and three dimensional [3d] imaging as well as road, aerial and birds eye views of a chosen location. This program is easy to use and effective. It provides clear, high quality images of a selected area. This program is highly recommended.

31. HULU, www.hulu.com

In the world of Internet, sometimes a program comes along that is labeled as a landmark program, given its innovation, and its ease of use. I believe that Hulu is such a program. Hulu provides, for FREE, a tremendous amount of formally commercially available, premium video. Hulu has over 50 available content providers including Fox, NBC, MGM, and others. Hulu offers both clips and FULL LENGTH episodes of past and current primetime TV shows, as well as full length, feature films. I found on Hulu such current series as Prison Break, in addition to some of the series that were popular in the 1950's and 1960's such as "McHale's Navy" and "Alfred Hitchcock Presents". Hulu is advertiser supported so there are a few short commercials in every program offered. I found Hulu to be both incredibly addictive and entertaining. The quality of Hulu content is equal to those offered commercially. It appears that Hulu is expanding its offerings rapidly and they even offer some proprietary content. Hulu is a MUST HAVE, TOP TEN SITE, AND IS HIGHLY RECOMMENDED!!

32. MODERNFEED, www.modernfeed.com

This is yet another site where network TV shows and other content are freely available. This site appears to have some similar content as Hulu and also some content that is different in scope such as "Star Trek" the original series. Modernfeed is a promising new service and should be monitored to see what content is made available through this service in the future.

I hope that the users/readers of this book will not only enjoy reading and viewing the book, but that they will be able to apply the information within, and gain a better understanding of the Internet. I also hope that users not only increased their knowledge - for their own edification- but to also increase their business acumen as well. I encourage all readers to contact me if they have any questions or comments to contact the author at epopkoff@ yahoo.com or through my publisher at www.spibooks.com. We both welcome your input. I also sincerely hope that all of your searches be fruitful, satisfying, and successful ones.

Appendix A
Websites of Interest by Category

Browsers

AOL Explorer, www.aol.com
Avant Browser, www.avantbrowser.com
Firefox 3.0, www.mozilla.com
Flock, www.flock.com
Internet Explorer, www.microsoft.com
Maxthon, www.maxthon.com
Opera 9, www.opera.com

Business and Stock Market Info

1st Headlines Business News, www.1stheadlines.com/business
Annual Report Service, www.annualreportservice.com
Big Charts, http://bigcharts.marketwatch.com
Bloomberg Investments Site, www.bloomberg.com
Briefing.com, www.briefing.com
Business Daily Review, http://businessdailyreview.com
Business Information on the Web, http://ils.unc.edu/nclibs/davidson/busres.htm
Business Wire, http://home.businesswire.com
CNBC, www.cnbc.com
CNN Money, http://money.cnn.com
Daily Stocks, www.dailystocks.com
EDGAR SCAN, http://edgarscan.pwcglobal.com/servlets/edgarscan
Fierce Finance, www.fiercefinance.com
Financial Week, www.financialweek.com
Financials.com, www.financials.com
Investment News, www.investmentnews.com
Investopedia, www.investopedia.com
Investor Calendar, www.investorcalendar.com
Investor Fact Sheet, www.investorfactsheets.com
Investor Links, www.investorlinks.com
Investors Business Daily, www.investors.com
Investorwords: Investing Glossary, www.investorwords.com

London Financial Times, ww.ft.com/home/us
MSN Money, http://moneycentral.msn.com/investo/home.asp
NASD Rules and Regulations, www.nasd.com/rulesregulation/index.htm
PR News Wire, www.companyreports.com
Reuter's Investor, www.reuters.com
SEC Filings, www.secfilings.com
SEC Info, www.secinfo.com
Securities and Exchange Commission, www.sec.gov
Stock Charts.com, www.stockcharts.com
Thomas Net, www.thomasnet.com
U.S. Stock Market, http://usstockmarket.com/index.asp
Yahoo Finance, http://finance.yahoo.com

Future of the Web/Web 2.0

411sync, www.411sync.com
Atlas, www.atlas.com
Avvenu, www.avvenu.com
CalendarHub, www.calendarhub.com
DOHOP, www.dohop.com
Ebuddy, www.ebuddy.com
Farecast, www.farecast.com
Flash Earth, www.flashearth.com
Free Webs, www.freewebs.com
Gigatribe, www.gigatribe.com
Google Docs & Spread Sheet, http:docs.google.com
HULU, ww.hulu.com
JOOPZ, www.joopz.com
JOTT, www.jott.com
Linked In, www.linkedin.com
MediaFire, www.mediafire.com
Meta Glossary, www.metaglossary.com
Microsoft Virtual Earth, www.microsoft.com/virtualearth
Microsoft Windows Live, www.windowslive.com
Mint, www.mint.com
ModernFeed, www.modernfeed.com
NeNest, www.nenest.com
Pandora, www.pandora.com

Pipl, www.pipl.com
Pxn8, www.pxn8.com
Relenta CRM, www.relentacrm.com
Scanr, www.scanr.com
Simply Hired, www.simplyhired.com
Spongecell, www.spongecell.com
Tape Failure, www.tapefailure.com
Think Free Office Online, www.thinkfree.com
Web 2 RSS, www.Web2rss.com
Yugma, www.yugma.com
ZOHO Office Suite, www.zoho.com
Zoom Info, www.zoominfo.com

Government and the Web

Ben's Guide to U.S. Government for Kids, http://bensguide.gpo.gov
Bureau of Economic Analysis, www.bea.gov
Bureau of Labor/Labor Stistics, www.bls.gov
Business Link to the U.S. Government, www.business.gov
Census Bureau, www.census.gov
Center for Disease Control & Prevention, www.cdc.gov
CIA: Central Intelligence Agency, www.cia.gov
Commodity Future Trading Commission, www.cftc.gov
Consumer Action Main Page, www.consumeraction.gov
Consumer Products Safety Commission, www.cpcs.gov
Department of Commerce, www.commerce.gov
Department of Energy, www.doe.gov
Department of Homeland Security, www.dhs.gov
Department of the Interior, www.doi.gov
Department of the Treasury, www.ustreas.gov
Department of Transportation, www.dot.gov
Department of Justice, www.justice.gov
Dept. of Commerce/Economic & Statistics Admin, www.esa.doc.gov
Development Publications, www.ntis.gov
Environmental Protection Agency (EPA), www.epa.gov
EPA/Enviromapper for Super Fund, www.epa.gov/enviro/sf
FBI: Federal Bureau of Investigation, www.fbi.gov
Fed World, www.fedworld.gov

Federal Aviation Administration, www.faa.gov
Federal Citizen Information Center, www.pueblo.gsa.gov
Federal Forms Catalog for Citizens, www.forms.gov
Federal Gov't Official Jobs Site, www.usajobs.gov
Federal Loan Information, www.govloans.gov
Federal Trade Commision, www.ftc.gov
Fedstats, www.Fedstats.gov
Food and Drug Administration, www.fda.gov
Food Safety Information, www.foodsafety.gov
Google U.S. Government Search, www.google.com/g/usgov
Government Printing Office, www.gpoaccess.gov
Government Grants, www.grants.gov
Gov't Sales: Merchandise, Real Estate, www.govsales.gov
Gov't Search Engine, www.searchgov.com
Hubble Space Telescope, http://hubble.nasa.gov
IRS: U.S. Internal Revenue Service, www.irs.gov
Library of Congress, www.loc.gov
Medline Plus: Health Infromation, www.medlineplus.gov
National Aeronautics & Space Administration, www.nasa.gov
National Atlas, www.nationalatlas.gov
National Map, www.nationalmap.gov
Nutrition Information, www.nutrition.gov
Online Resource for Recalls, www.recalls.gov
Planetary Photo Journal, http://photojournal.ipl.nasa.gov
Recreation Maps, www.recreationmaps.gov
Securities and Exchange Commission, www.sec.gov
Small Business Administration, www.sba.gov
Social Security, www.ssa.gov
State Department, www.state.gov
State Department/Travel, http://travel.state.gov
State Master, www.statemaster.com
State, County, City Websites, www.statelocalgov.net
Stat-USA/Internet, www.stat-usa.gov
Thomas, http://thomas.lov.gov
U.S. Computer Emergency Readiness Team, www.us-cert.gov
U.S. Consumer Product Safety Council, www.cpsc.gov
U.S. Financial Literacy & Education Commission, www.mymoney.gov
U.S. Government Information, www.usa.gov
U.S. Patent and Trademark Office, http://patents.uspto.gov

U.S. Postal Service (USPS), www.usps.gov
Whirlwind Project, http://whirlwind.arc.nasa.gov
White House, www.whitehouse.gov
Your Benefits Connection, www.govbenefits.gov

International News Service

Babel Fish Translation, http://babelfish.altavista.com
BBC World News Service, http://news.bbc.co.uk
CAROL: Company Annual Reports Online, www.carol.co.uk
EIN News: The World News Monitor, www.einnews.com
International Investing, www.wall-street.com/foreign.html
Numberway: The Free White Pages, www.numberway.com
Pressdisplay 350 Newspapers from 65 Countries, www.pressdisplay.com
Reuter's Online, http://today.reuters.com/news/home.aspx
Stock Markets of the World, www.escapeartist.com/stock/markets.htm
Wayp: International White and Yellow Pages, www.wayp.com
World Top News Stories, www.worldtopnews.com
Worldpress.org, www.worldpress.org
Xanadu, www.foreignword.com

International Resources

BBC News, http://news.bbc.co.uk/2/hi/country_profiles/default.stm
IDB Summary of Demographic Data, www.census.gov/ipc/www/idb
International Monetary Fund, www.imf.org.external/data.htm
Language Resource Online, www.languageresourceonline.com
Nation Master, www.nationmaster.com/index.php
Search Engine Colossus, wwwsearchenginecolossus.com
Site-by-Site Investment Portal & Research Center, www.site-by-site.com
Spire Project: Country Profiles, http://spireproject.com/country.htm
U.N. Cartographic Section, www.un.org/depts/cartographic/english/htmain.htm
U.S. Dept. of State Background Notes, www.state.gov/r/pa/ei/bgn
U.S. Dept. of State, Country, Commercial Guides Index, www.state.gov/www/about_state/business/com_guides/index.html
UN Cyberschoolbus, http://cyberschoolbus.un.org

Invisible Web

Copernic, www.copernic.com
Incywincy, www.incywincy.com
U.S. Gov't Search System, www.usa.gov

Library-Based Search Systems

Amazon, www.amazon.com
Answers, www.answers.com
Argali White and Yellow, www.argali.com
Bartleby, www.bartleby.com
CEO Express, www.ceoexpress.com
Complete Planet, www.completeplanet.com
Congoo Netpass, www.congoo.com
Individual, www.individual.com
Infomine, http://infomine.ucr.edu
Librarian's Index to the Internet, www.lii.org
Library Thing, www.librarything.com
Magportal, www.magportal.com
NewsNose, www.newsnose.com
OAIster, www.Oaister.org
Questia, www.questia.com
Refdesk, www.refdesk.com
The Internet Public Library, www.IPL.org

Library Electronic Resources

ABI Inform Research, www.brooklynpubliclibrary.org
Academic Search Premiere, www.brooklynpubliclibrary.org
Accunet/AP Photo Archive, www.queenslibrary.org
African American Experience, www.queenslibrary.org
America the Beautiful, www.brooklynpubliclibrary.org
America's Newspapers, www.denverlibrary.org
America's Obituaries and Death Notices, www.denverlibrary.org
Ancient and Medieval History Online, www.nypl.org
Art Museum Image Gallery, www.bpl.org

Associations Unlimited, www.brooklynpubliclibrary.org
Bowker's Books in Print, www.queenslibrary.org
Biography and Genealogy Master Index, www.queenslibrary.org
Biography Reference Bank, www.brooklynpubliclibrary.org
Book Index with Reviews, www.brooklynpubliclibrary.org
Books in Print.com Professional, www.brooklynpubliclibrary.org
Boston Globe, Historical 1872-1923, www.bpl.org
Boston Public Library/Boston, Massachusetts, www.bpl.org
Brooklyn Public Library, www.brooklynpubliclibrary.org
Business and Company ASAP, www.queenslibrary.org
Business and Company Resource Center, www.brooklynpubliclibrary.org
Business and Management Practices, www.bpl.org
Business Source Premiere, www.brooklynpubliclibrary.org
Children's Literature Comprehensive Database, www.queenslibrary.org
College Source Online, www.queenslibrary.org
Columbia Gazetteer of the World: Online, www.nypl.org
Computer Database, www.spl.org
Corporate Resource Net, www.brooklynpubliclibrary.org
Credo Reference, www.brooklynpubliclibrary.org
Culture Grams, www.nassaulibrary.org
Culture Grams Online, www.spl.org
Custom Newspapers, www.brooklynpubliclibrary.org
D and B Million Dollar Database, www.bpl.org
Denver Public Library Online, www.denverlibrary.org
Dictionary of Literacy, www.nypl.org
Digital Sanborn Maps, www.spl.org
Early American Newspapers, Series 1 & 2/1690-1819, www.bpl.org
Ebsco Animals, www.queenslibrary.org
Encyclopedia Americana, www.brooklynpubliclibrary.org
Encyclopedia Britannica, www.brooklynpubliclibrary.org
ERIC, www.brooklynpubliclibrary.org
Freguson's Career Guidance Center, www.brooklynpubliclibrary.org
Funk & Wagneall's New World Encyclopedia, www.queenslibrary.org
Gale Virtual Reference Library, www.brooklynpubliclibrary.org
Global Books in Print.com, www.queenslibrary.org
Google Book Search, http://books.google.com/googleprint/library.html
Health Reference Center Academic, www.brooklynpubliclibrary.org
Health Source Consumer Edition, www.brooklynpubliclibrary.org
History Reference Center, www.brooklynpubliclibrary.org

History Resources Center, www.nypl.org
Informe, www.brooklynpubliclibrary.org
Infotrac Student Edition/K-12, www.queenslibrary.org
Integrum Worldwide, www.queenslibrary.org
Investext Plus, www.nassaulibrary.org
Land and Peoples Online, ww.brooklynpubliclibrary.org
Lawchek Online, www.queenslibrary.org
Learning Express Library, www.brooklynpubliclibrary.org
Library Literature, www.nypl.org
Library Literature & Information Science, www.brooklynpubliclibrary.org
Literary Reference Center, www.brooklynpubliclibrary.org
Litfinder, www.queenslibrary.org
MasterFile Premiere, www.brooklynpubliclibrary.org
McClatchy Tribune Collection, www.brooklynpubliclibrary.org
Mergent FIS Online, www.brooklynpubliclibrary.org
Middle Search Plus, www.brooklynpubliclibrary.org
Modern World History Online, www.nypl.org
Morning Star, www.denverlibrary.org
Nassau Library System, www.nassaulibrary.org
National Newspaper Index, www.brooklynpubliclibrary.org
Natural Medicines Database, www.brooklynpubliclibrary.org
New Book of Knowledge, www.brooklynpubliclibrary.org
New Book of Popular Science, www.brooklynpubliclibrary.org
New York Public Library, www.nypl.org
New York State Newspapers, www.brooklynpubliclibrary.org
New York Times, www.brooklynpubliclibrary.org
Newspaper Source, www.brooklynpubliclibrary.org
Novelist, www.brooklynpubliclibrary.org
Nueva Enciclopedia Cumbre en Linea, www.brooklynpubliclibrary.org
Opposing Viewpoints Resource Center, www.queenslibrary.org
Press Display, www.spl.org
Primary Search, www.brooklynpubliclibrary.org
Professional Development Collection, www.brooklynpubliclibrary.org
Proquest Historical Newspapers, www.nassaulibrary.org
Psychology & Behavioral Science Collection, www.nypl.org
Queens Library System, www.queenslibrary.org
Questia, www.questia.com
Rare Books, www.bpl.org
Reference USA, www.brooklynpubliclibrary.org

Regional Business News, www.brooklynpubliclibrary.org
Rosetta Stone, www.denverlibrary.org
Rosetta Stone Online Language Learning Center, www.nypl.org
Safari Books Online, www.spl.org
Science Online, www.nypl.org
Science Resource Center, www.brooklynpubliclibrary.org
Searchasaurus, www.queenslibrary.org
Seattle Public Library, Seattle Washington, www.spl.org
Serials Directory, www.brooklynpubliclibrary.org
SIRS Discover on the Web, www.queenslibrary.org
SIRS Knowledge Source, www.queenslibrary.org
Smithsonian Global Sound, www.denverlibrary.org
Standard and Poor's Net Advantage, www.queenslibrary.org
Student Resource Center, www.brooklynpubliclibrary.org
Student Resource Center Silver, www.queenslibrary.org
Table Base, www.bpl.org
The Online Books, http://digital.library.upenn.edu/books
Thompson Gale Legal Forms, www.nassaulibrary.org
Twaynes Author's Series, www.brooklynpubliclibrary.org
Ulrichs Periodical Directory, www.spl.org
Value Line Investment Survey, www.denverlibrary.org
Washington State News Stand, www.spl.org
World Book Online Encyclopedia, www.queenslibrary.org

Miscellaneous

AOL.com, www.aol.com
Bellarc Computer Inventory Program, www.bellarc.com
Copernic Desktop Search, www.copernic.com
Desktop Sidebar, www.desktopsidebar.com
DriverMax, www.download.com
Esnips.com, www.esnips.com
Freebiz Magazine, www.freebizmag.com
Feed43, http://feed43.com
First Stop Web Search Standard Edition, www.firststopWebsearch.com
Mail 2 Web, www.mail2Web.com
Netsnippets Free Edition, www.netsnippets.com/basic/index.htm
Open Office, www.openoffice.org

Side Step Travel, www.sidestep.com
SIW System Information Tool, www.download.com
Snap Files Pro, www.snapfilespro.com
Stickies5.2b, www.zhornsoftware.co.uk/stickies
Stumble Upon, www.download.com
The Google Pack, www.google.com
Zone Alarm Free Firewall, www.zonelabs.com

News Aggregator

ABC News Homepage, http://abcnews.go.com
AmphetaDesk, www.disobey.com/amphetadesk
Associated Press (AP) News Wire, www.ap.org
Awasu Personal Edition, www.awasu.com
Blogbridge, www.blogbridge.com
Bloglines, www.bloglines.com
CNN.com, www.cnn.com
Crayon.net, www.crayon.net
Eufees, www.eufeeds.eu
FeedDemon, www.feeddemon.com
Feedster, www.feedster.com
Free Byte News Central, www.freebyte.com/news
Google Video, www.video.google.com
Google Alerts, www.google.com/alerts
Headline Spot, www.headlinespot.com
Individual.com, www.individual.com
Interactive Museum of News, www.newseum.org
Internet Archive, www.archive.org
Internet Public Library Newspaper Area, www.ipl.org/div/news
Media Channel: Guide of Internet, TV, and Video, www.mediachannel.
com
MSNBC, www.MSNBC.com
My News Bot, www.mynewsbot.com
National Feed Room, www.national.feedroom.com
Newplorer, www.newsplorer.com
News Index, www.newsindex.com
News is Free, Your Personal News Portal, www.newsisfree.com
News on Feeds, www.newsonfeeds.com/faq/aggregators

NewsNose, www.download.com
Newspapers 24, www.newspapers24.com
Newspapers.com, www.newspapers.com
Newz.info, www.newz.info
NewzCrawler, www.newzcrawler.com
Online Newspapers, www.onlinenewspapers.com
Online Newspapers, www.allyoucanread.com
Paper of Record, www.paperofrecord.com
Pluck, www.pluck.com
Real Networks, www.real.com
Refdesk Newspapers USA and Worldwide, www.refdesk.com/paper.htm
Rocketinfo, www.rocketnews.com
Search Video, www.searchvideo.com
Small Town Newspapers, www.smalltownpapers.com
Syndic8, www.syndic8.com
Topix, www.topix.net
U.S. News Archives, www.ibiblio.org/slanews/internet/archives.html
United Press International, www.upi.com
USA Today, www.usatoday.com
World Newspapers and Magazines, www.world-newspapers.com
World Wide Newspapers, www.newspapersonline.info
Yahoo Video, http://video.search.yahoo
You Tube, www.youtube.com

Public Information

Argali White and Yellow, www.argali.com
BRB's Free Resource Center, www.brbpub.com/pubrecsites.asp?h=1
Federal Bureau of Prisons, www.bop.gov
Free Law Links, www.freelawlinks.com
National Archives and Records Administration, www.archives.gov
Reference USA, www.referenceusa.com
Search Systems, www.searchsystems.net
The Black Book Online, www.blackbookonline.info
Yellowpages 411, www.411locate.com
Zoom Info, ww.zoominfo.com

Search Engines

Ask, www.ask.com
Carrot Clustering Engine, www.carrot2.org
Clusty, www.clusty.com
Cometquery, www.cometquery.com
Dogpile, www.dogpile.com
Flexfinder, www.flexfinder.com
Gigablast, www.gigablast.com
Google, www.google.com/g/usgov
Graball, www.graball.com
Grokker Metasearch, www.grokker.com
I Seek, www.iseek.com
iBoogie, www.iboogie.com
Incywincy, www.incywincy.com
Ixquick, www.ixquick.com
Kartoo, www.kartoo.com
Mamma, www.mamma.com
MSN Search, www.msn.com
Nextaris Metasearch, www.nextaris.com
Qksearch, www.qksearch.com
Surfwax, www.surfwax.com
Yahoo, www.yahoo.com

Toolbars and Add Ons

Activeshopper, www.activeshopper.com
Alexa, www.alexa.com
Answers.com, www.answers.com
AOL, http://downloads.channel.aol.com/toolbar
Clusty, www.clusty.com/toolbar
Congoo Net Pass, www.congoo.com
Dogpile, www.dogpile.com
Earthlink, www.earthlink.net/software/free/toolbar
Fox News, www.infospace.com/info.foxnws/tbar
Google, http://toolbar.msn.com
Groowe, .www.groowe.com
MapQuest, www.mapquest.com

Merriam Webster, www.m-w.com
Reel New Media, http://reelnewmedia.communitytoolbars.com
Stumble Upon, www.stumbleupon.com
UCMore, www.ucmore.com
Wikisearch, en.wikipedia.org/wiki/toolbar
Windows Live, http://toolbar.live.com
Wizz RSS News Reader, www.wizzcomputers.com/wizzrss.php
Yahoo Companion, http://toolbar.yahoo.com

Weather Information Services

ACCUWeather.com, www.accuweather.com
Find Local Weather, www.findlocalweather.com
National Oceanic & Atmospheric Administration, www.noaa.gov
National Weather Service, www.weather.gov
The Weather Channel, www.weather.com
The Weather Underground, www.wunderground.com
UM Weather, http://cirrus.sprl.umich.edu/wxnet
Weather Bug, www.weatherbug.com

Appendix B
Page Index